EMBRACING OUR ESSENCE

Embracing *Our* Essence

Spiritual Conversations *with* Prominent Women

SUSAN SKOG &

Betty Ford ✦ Naomi Judd ✦ Marian Wright Edelman ✦ Betty Eadie
Joan Borysenko ✦ Sophy Burnham ✦ Elisabeth Kubler-Ross
Susan Ford Bales ✦ Nikki Giovanni ✦ Ada Deer ✦ Ardath Rodale
Terry Tempest Williams ✦ Alexandra Stoddard
Madeleine L'Engle ✦ Nell Newman ✦ Rachel Naomi Remen
Marilyn Ferguson ✦ Elizabeth Roberts ✦ Mary Jacksteit
Adrienne Kaufmann ✦ Corinne McLaughlin ✦ Dawn English
Frances Vaughan ✦ Joan Halifax ✦ Bonnie Steinberg
Jane Goodall ✦ Joan B. Campbell ✦ Christiane Northrup
Linda Caldwell Fuller

Health Communications, Inc.
Deerfield Beach, Florida

Grateful acknowledgment is made to the following for permission to reprint from:

Guide My Feet, by Marian Wright Edelman, © 1995 by Marian Wright Edelman. Reprinted by permission of Beacon Press.

"River of Time" by Naomi Judd and John Jarvis, © 1989 Kentucky Sweetheart Music/Cross Keys Music. All rights reserved. Used by permission.

ISBN 1-55874-359-6

Publisher: Health Communications, Inc.
3201 S.W. 15th Street
Deerfield Beach, Florida 33442-8190

Cover design by Andrea Perrine Brower
Author photo by Ray Congrove, Photographic Developments, Davenport, Iowa
Cover photograph, © LIFESTOCK, Anthony Beaverson

This book is dedicated to our children, all over the world, affected by AIDS. A portion of the author's royalties will be given to organizations that care for children with AIDS.

Contents

Acknowledgments

I begin with my affection and gratitude to Alexandra Stoddard, Joan Borysenko and Betty Eadie for their kindness and encouragement as the book first germinated.

My highest praise for all the special and talented people at Health Communications who recognized the destiny of this book and went the extra mile to make it a reality. I especially extend my gratitude to my publishers Peter Vegso and Gary Seidler for their vision and business acumen; my editor Christine Belleris for her keen belief in the book, editorial savvy and personal support; communications director Kim Weiss for her creative drive, expertise and friendship; and editor Matthew Diener for his astute insights and editorial talents. To Nancy Burke, I thank you immensely for helping shepherd the book in its final stages. Thanks also to Lee Swanson for his art direction in finalizing the design of the cover.

To my friends Ann, Susan, Beth, Doreen, Carleen, Marla,

Carol, Tanya and Annie: your support came at critical moments and meant the world. A special thank-you to Fred Edmonds and Lana Hoff, who always affirmed the merit of my spiritual seekings. Finally, my deepest affection and thanks to my husband, Jim; my sons, Jeffrey and Evan; my parents, Bob and Vivian Stuekerjuergen; my husband's parents, Clarence and Jean Skog; and my sisters Ann Garmager and Joan Conrad for their strength, inspiration and injections of humor when most needed.

Introduction

Our spirituality is our opening to one another as whole human beings, each different and precious, and our exploring how we can truly learn to love.

—Jean Grasso Fitzpatrick

Women ablaze with spiritual goodness and purpose are transforming and healing our world as never before. Millions of us are embracing—or may be just on the verge of discovering— our spiritual essence—our intuitiveness, wisdom, resilience and compassion. We are awakening from a spirit-less somnolence to see our relationships, society, environment, children, institutions and, most important, ourselves in a startling new spiritual context.

Infused, even exhilarated with our individual and collective abilities to shine, we finally see we can indeed create a new world. We don't have to wait for the ubiquitous "them" to do something. We are "them," and we are already deep into shaping a more loving and humane reality. At the same time, we fully realize the only way we can carve out this courageous new existence is by first nourishing our very souls. A rich new external world must spring from our lush interiors. We must lay a loving foundation in our own hearts and spirits before we can build soulful communities around us. Anything else is an illusion.

We see greater spirituality, then, as our only hope for soul satisfaction—and our society's best hope for evolution. Which is why, after years of seeking solace in worldly distractions, shallow relationships, career kudos and materialistic binges, unprecedented numbers of us are on full-blown inner quests, knowing fully that we will encounter unfamiliar, even terrifying territory.

For our spiritual growth is inevitably linked to intensely personal, often painful awakenings. We begin to awaken as we admire our meticulously decorated homes and whisper, "There has to be something more." One day, as we watch our children sleep, or smell the air after a rainstorm—or get a dreaded prognosis about our health—we sense our souls irreparably shift. We can almost feel our souls gasp as something new is born. And in that soul-shift, we feel an intense connection to something greater than ourselves and a new, raw concern for humanity everywhere. As German mystic Meister Eckhart said, "Whatever God does, the first outburst is always compassion." We feel alternately electrified—and humbled—by the palpable sense that we are exquisitely wrought, lovingly planned and molded for a Divine purpose. We have been sent here with gifts of insight, talents, goodness and light to create a better world.

When did my own spiritual stirrings begin? When did I first sense the world in a different, deeper way? Much of it began growing up in the magical Iowa countryside, in a child's ultimate delight of dense woods, streams running with crayfish and guppies, and bushes heavy with raspberries and gooseberries. In a world where towering oaks, maples, hickories and locusts gave life to my dreams and dance to my imagination. I credit my parents with intuitively knowing how healthy it was to allow my four siblings and me to roam free in the woods, playing hide-and-seek on frozen creekbeds, poking in hollow trees, burying ourselves in autumn leaves or pouncing on the first bluebells of spring.

I think it is indeed possible for a child to first experience a Higher Power through mud, water and tree limbs, and many of us fortunate enough to come of age in such a wild place are evidence of it. The woods were—and still are—the most gloriously crafted sanctuary I can think of, where one can lie down in and gain strength from the life there, not knowing or caring, really, where the body ends and the spirit begins. Not listening to the chatter of the mind but to the whisper of the wind in the changing leaves.

As a teenager, I spent countless nights searching the night sky, wondering what was really "out there." A hunger to connect with something greater than myself was largely fed through time in the woods and by keeping a journal in thick sky-blue ink of my own and others' thoughts, from Thoreau to Greek philosophers. In 1969, when Neil Armstrong and Buzz Aldrin first walked on the moon, millions of us vicariously felt as if we too were glimpsing our first real gateway to infinity. The Apollo 11 mission made such an impression on me that for years I lined the bottoms of my dresser drawers with newspaper clippings and pictures of that first incredible closeup of the lunar landscape.

My spiritual evolution lurched forward, roughly and painfully, almost four years ago. Like many women featured in my book, a physical degeneration was the abrupt catalyst for spiritual regeneration. Almost overnight, I began having searing pain from my fingertips to my shoulders. An MRI showed several ruptured discs in my neck, the result of normal degeneration over the years.

One gray January morning I awoke from surgery to feel myself encased in a head-to-shoulder brace after the removal of the discs and a spinal fusion. Unable to walk much, drive, or talk more than a whisper for weeks because of damaged vocal cords, I retreated from the outside world—and ultimately went deep within. During long winter days, I turned to writings of the heart, from those of Thoreau to Rainer Maria Rilke, Anne Morrow Lindbergh to Alexandra Stoddard. For two years after, I continued to wander through Hebrew teachings, Buddhist tracts, Christian mysticism, metaphysical philosophies, Native American prayers and Islamic poems.

Last winter, my explorations seized center stage. No glorious, shining debut. It was akin to waking up, looking around, finding oneself barreling ahead on an unplanned journey—and panic!—"I never said goodbye to the old life! What do I take along? Where do I get off?"

As much as I tried to return to the status quo, I couldn't shake the sense of aching for something else and of constantly hearing an incessant, unyielding inner voice telling me to wake up. Stop doing, quit whirling, listen quietly and be ready for what was to come next. As much as I tried to maintain the normal flow of our days, I felt restless, raw, even anguished, not fully understanding the rapid inner transformation causing me to chafe at my outer life.

My reading became a feverish, almost obsessive thing. The words of timeless "souljourners," from Hildegard of Bingen to Buddah, from Jesus to Gandhi, from Teresa of Avila to Lao Tzu, and from Socrates to Albert Einstein, brought immense relief. "Ah, now I see. . . ." At the same time, I was increasingly saddened by our neglect of children, unethical ways of doing business, gross abuse of the environment, materialistic appetite and intolerance of differences.

I began to spend more hours alone, in nature, trying to stay receptive to any Divine assistance and inspiration available. I spent time just sitting at the computer, simply waiting for my next "assignment." When I finally quieted life down, made no plans and just stayed open, I began to experience electrifying moments I can only conclude were of a spiritual nature. I began to wake at 5 A.M. to meditate, think, pray or to merely savor the solitude before my family woke. One morning while meditating, I experienced the classic sensation—described in multitudes of cultures for millions of years—of being enveloped, enfolded and energized by a pure white light. No longer able to feel my physical body in any form, I saw that I had come from and was forever part of the light. It is no minor coincidence that all religious traditions uniformly speak of our origin in the light.

And I finally saw that my months of seeking were not aimless, that they indeed had purpose and worth. I sensed that I could always depend on and be uplifted by this intense source of love and light. I felt anguished, thinking, "But I don't want to leave you." And I distinctly heard the message, "You never have to."

St. Augustine once wrote, "I entered and beheld with the eye of my soul . . . above my mind, light unchangeable. . . . He that knows the truth, knows what that light is; and he that knows it, knows eternity." I was beginning to have some sense of what the light was. And I knew there was no turning back to my old way of seeing. The journey was unfolding.

I began to better understand the rich history—and quiet confidence—of those who relied more on the Divine, often mysterious strength available to us all. They showed we have unfathomable, inexhaustible power to do good in the world, and that we are constantly supported and surrounded by Divine assistance in choosing to live more humanely. Whatever you wish to call the source of all creation—God, Yahweh, the Absolute, Allah, the Divine Mother, the Source, the One, the "Love that loved us into existence," as St. Augustine described the Divine—our Higher Power knows our most intimate desires and guides our lives in ways far grander than our wildest imaginations.

Yet as sure as I am of these spiritual truths, I continue to wrestle with so many other questions. I'm not as compassionate, patient and nonjudgmental as I want to be. I certainly don't freely welcome pain and conflict as succor for my spiritual growth. And as much as I try, it is so hard to see the sacred in cleaning up entrails of my children's spaghetti from the floor.

And what are we all actually longing for, experiencing, going toward? Why is the spiritual pull so strong? Caught up in the stuff of life, what daily practices can we weave into our days to further jump-start our spiritual growth? Don't we all wonder how we can live more peacefully and purposefully in a troubled world?

I came to believe millions of us, women and men alike, are increasingly asking these questions. One December night sitting by a fire, I wondered out loud to my husband what it would be like to tap the wisdom of more experienced female spiritual seekers and gain some frame of reference for my own wonderings. "Wouldn't it be great if I could talk with Joan Borysenko about her experiences with meditation, mind-body issues and other spiritual stuff?" To me, Borysenko is truly a modern-day mystic, and for years I'd found her books incredibly insightful and intuitive. The next evening, I turned on a television program on PBS and started laughing when I saw Joan Borysenko talking about the power of prayer. The narrator said Borysenko had recently moved from the East Coast to the mountains outside of Boulder, Colorado—one hour from my home! And in yet another instant of divinely inspired clarity—not chance or coincidence—I knew that my book's journey would be launched in the coming year.

And so it was, and so I share it with all of you as we move forward together in cultivating our lush interior. I have been overwhelmingly grateful for and forever inspired by the compassion, empathy, humor, strength and wisdom of those I've interviewed. They are superb spiritual role models for all of us, women and men, as we embrace new, more fulfilling ways of living. They can help us cope with the dark nights of the soul that invariably lie ahead. They can help us see clearly the spiritual truths that will bring more personal meaning to our days and illuminate our world.

Here are 10 of these truths that echoed over and over again, like a spiritual symphony, from the women I interviewed:

We are literally, concretely, vitally connected to one another and with a Higher Power. This is not metaphorical, poetic or philosophical. This is a timeless idea that pervades all the major traditions. Because of this connectedness, what is done to one of us is done to us all. Any loving acts send out loving reverberations in the world, just as our hateful words, thoughts and acts spread a mean-spirited malignancy. Knowing of this connectedness, then, behooves us to love and care for one another better—humans and nonhumans alike.

Just as we are, we are intensely, innately spiritual. We are living sparks of divinity with the power to light the world. Our true natures are sacred, good and ever so wise. God permeates our every atom, cell and thought. We don't have to do anything, be anything or go anywhere because we are all naturally part of a universal rhythm, flow, balance, dance. We just have to remember we are part of the One, a feather on the breath of God, as Hildegard of Bingen wrote.

Respecting and caring for ourselves is the first critical step toward connecting with the Absolute. Feeding our own souls should become as practical and natural as brushing our teeth, washing our faces and toning our bodies. Because we are all seamlessly connected, going within to find more harmony is never selfish or self-centered—it delivers much-needed peace to the world. Only by changing ourselves, person by person, will we change the world. Taking responsibility for our lives—knowing our limits, communicating our boundaries, saying "no" to too many demands—cherishes our sacred selves and restores us to our fullness. Strengthening our spiritual sinews provides the strength to go about the outer work needed in the world. Thus, we have the right to avoid situations, people and events that destroy our peace of mind, body and soul. Only when we replenish our own spirits, regularly and without guilt, can we be resilient enough to love the terminally ill, the children, the homeless or the environment.

We have devalued, underestimated and failed to call on the immense spiritual support available to and within all of us. We don't have to tough it out alone in this life. We don't have to feel frightened and vulnerable all the time. We can learn to live more in the present moment, not regretting the past, not fearing the future. **We can actively visualize God's love surrounding us and others**

in need. We can close our eyes and imagine Divine light and love healing our violent cities, cleansing our polluted selves, skies and streams, surrounding and protecting our children, all over the world. We can ask for help and receive it. From the moment we arrive on earth, we are enfolded, literally bathed in the support of a Higher Power, angels, spiritual guides and more love and light than we could ever imagine. All we have to do is ask. All we need to do is let the light and wisdom from within break our bonds of flesh and reach outward. We are not powerless. Far from it. We are filled with an immense power for beauty and goodness.

We won't hear our spirit's call if we constantly drown it out with incessant activity. We need moments of absolute stillness to quiet our mind's chatter and let our souls stretch and speak to us. We won't hear the voice inside us and allow it to guide our lives if we insist on blasting through our days nonstop. Without solitude, wrote author Anne Morrow Lindbergh, we spill our time, energy and creativity without letting the pitcher fill to the brim. Without quiet, says Marian Wright Edelman, we can't hear the sound of "the genuine" within each of us.

The spiritual is not found in the grandiose, the magnificent, the ostentatious display. It is found in the ordinary moments, in the preparation and sharing of a meal, in the unfolding of a lilac bush outside your window, in a child's sigh, in a conflict with a coworker, in the passing of a parent. Miracles happen daily if we have the eyes to see them. Anything that makes us more aware of our connections with one another and all of creation and helps us love deeply is spiritual.

Spiritual serenity is not the exclusive domain of any one tradition, religion or practice. We each find God in our own way because God is within and all around us. No book, no worship service, no intellectual doctrine can substitute for our own experience of the Divine. Religious rituals, hymn singing, group meditations or candle lighting can powerfully connect us with a Higher Power, but they are only conduits, not divinity itself.

Suffering and the timeless dark nights of the soul are a necessary, maybe unavoidable, prelude to the ultimate odyssey—our journey within. For it is in suffering that our souls open to something new, and our reverence and appreciation for all things is deepened. Through suffering and loss, we can often find the jewel in the lotus of the heart, as Buddhists describe it. Our vulnerability in suffering teaches us how to love like few lessons really can.

Becoming more spiritual doesn't miraculously shield us from future suffering. Nothing safeguards or buffers us totally from crisis. **But a faith in a Higher Power can help us absorb the blows of life and find some inner peace.** If we didn't suffer, how would we feel deeper compassion for others' pain?

With spiritual growth comes a sense of humility and surrender to our creator, the loving force that knows our most intimate dreams and desires and guides our lives in ways far greater than our grandest fantasies. Literally sensing and trusting that force, even when it seems totally illogical, will take our lives to heights we've scarcely imagined, if at all. Meditating to quiet our internal talk and instead amplify God's voice and energy can transform our body, mind and spirits as never before. Depending on a Higher Power—and praying out loud, regularly, on our knees, in our cars, as we bathe our children—may be the wisest, most pragmatic thing we will ever do. "Thy will be done" is not an old-fashioned notion—it is as profound and as comforting as it gets.

Finally, the women featured in this book warmly affirm what we have always known inside: that from the moment we arrived on earth, we were meant to live more lovingly, purposefully and simply. That we must be catalysts for change. That we have a responsibility to transform our world. That we do indeed have a gloriously larger destiny that extends far beyond the boundaries of our towns, countries and this physical plane. These women show us that life is meant to be literally flooded with simple wonders and quiet joys. We are meant to celebrate and protect nature—and each other.

I hope their messages give us all the inner courage and outer resolve to heed their collective wisdom and move forward on the most engrossing and captivating journey of our lives.

ELIZABETH ROBERTS

Ecological teacher,
author and consultant

*"If we have a moral obligation in these times, it is to
be joyful in the face of what we know. We are called
to be hospice workers at the beds of dying
institutions and cultures. But we are also called
to be midwives for what is being born."*

In the late 1980s, Elizabeth Roberts was propelled into her third decade as a respected and effective philosopher, teacher and social activist. She'd championed women's issues, fought for human rights with Martin Luther King, crusaded for fair housing and spearheaded television reform. She'd coordinated a White House conference on children and youth and was a former program director for National Public Radio, an assistant to John D. Rockefeller III and the associate dean of women at Marquette University. In addition, she was working on her doctorate and raising a daughter by herself.

And Roberts was exhausted. Tired of hurtling through life without feeling its textures. Tired of pushing a body weakened by malaria, back surgery and Chronic Fatigue Syndrome. Soul-sick from ignoring that quiet, but increasingly insistent, voice inside.

"I was burned out, in part because I had no sustaining contemplative practice. I had loads of physical energy and I thought life was about doing as much as you can. Doing everything the boys were doing, but doing it faster, better and with a baby on your back. That was the feminist ideology of the 70s and early 1980s, and it didn't begin to occur to many of us until we got sick that this was a lousy model. Why were we copying it? No one should live this way."

When Roberts' sickness finally forced her to stop, her inner voice rose and swelled like a long-dormant song to orchestrate her new life. "My body's sickness was actually the earth's sickness calling through me. I felt intuitively that what's going on in inside our own bodies is directly related to what's happening with the earth."

For nine months Roberts lived at a Sufi community in rural England. It was during this time that she took part in the spiritual death and rebirth of her self. Her renewal was guided by Sufi master and psychotherapist, Murshid Fazal Inayat-Khan, and her partner, Elias Amidon. During this period of solitude, Roberts discovered a greater spiritual depth to her already fierce social activism. Physically debilitated, she remained in bed and was unable to write or read for long periods. She began to meditate and live in her right brain, as she describes it. And she slowly began to collect material for *Earth Prayers From Around the World: 365 Prayers, Poems and Invocations for Honoring the Earth*, a unique collection of universal prayers from all traditions celebrating the sacredness and wisdom of the earth.

"That's all I could do. I told my partner, 'I don't know how to stop. I've always felt it was my job to fix the world. That's what I have been doing for 20 years.' And he said, 'Pray.' And I said, 'Pray? I don't know how to pray. I don't know whom to pray to.'

"And we began to talk about the fact that there must be a kind of prayer that reminds you of the story of the universe unfolding. So I began to look for people who had that kind of voice."

Earth Prayers became the first of Roberts' books, lectures and workshops to celebrate the spiritual wonder of the natural world.

Roberts' personal experience is a classic example of how greater creativity, conviction and a sense of our true calling to life often spring forth from the darkest periods of suffering. Yet our society ignores, even ridicules, our need to feel our spiritual grief and our pain, to heal, be still, listen, search and slowly evolve.

"We don't live in a society that rewards the quiet time, the receptive time, the not-knowing time, the chaotic, dark winter in which the seeds get regenerated before they push up into spring. That requires incredible strength. Our culture is a runaway caricature of masculine values. It is in full summer all the time and has no understanding of our cyclical nature or our need for a turning inward and reflection, as well as our need for a time of outward energy and life."

After her intensive spiritual retreat, Roberts made some major life changes. She sold her home in Cambridge, moved to Boulder, Colorado, got rid of her television, stopped driving and now lives a simpler but much richer life. A student of Thich Nhat Hanh's path of engaged Buddhism and creation spirituality, Roberts weaves Christian and Buddhist teachings together in her classes and workshops. She teaches at the Naropa Institute in Boulder and is chairwoman of the Institute for Deep Ecology. She is a frequent guide for wilderness and desert retreats.

"Because I felt my body was heeding the earth's call, I also began to turn my attention to environmental activism, recognizing that our deepest environmental problems are manifested in our spiritual life." Roberts now has embarked on new books, conferences and initiatives to help us all heed the earth's call and save the planet from technological and material excess. She is the coeditor of *Honoring the Earth*, and most recently, *The Earth and Her People* and the upcoming *The Soul of the City*.

A regular meditator, Roberts regards her main spiritual practice as daily living—ever mindful of the need to serve. "We need to understand that spirit is not confined to a cathedral, an altar, or a practice. It's just there whenever I'm able to connect with it. So my main practice is to slow way down whether I'm talking to you, or playing with a child, or writing a book, or organizing a demonstration, or making a meal.

"First I have to slow way down, and then I can tune into the relationships around me. And that relationship is one of listening, emptying and not figuring out all the answers by myself. The whole universe is working with us."

She first began hearing the earth when she was a little girl seeking the solace of trees, Roberts says. Now, her focus is to help others understand the earth call that beckons them as the natural world tries to rebalance itself from environmental abuse.

The call is what goes on when the kids are in bed, the lists are all put aside, the telephone has been turned down, you have a cup of tea, your feet are up and something is still pulling at your soul. For each one of us, the call will be different.

And I want to tell you, that when you are feeling those things pulling at your soul, that is the earth communicating to you. That is the earth talking through you. And what that means in concrete, ecological terms is that the earth's priorities are expressing themselves through your most personal, psychological and spiritual concerns. And the earth's call for a new way, for release from the pressures of the consumer and industrial society, is our own inner call for a way of life and a pace that's nourishing. That's why the sickness I had was so painful. It was the only way to stop me. That's why so many of us are physically suffering during our dark night of the soul journeys. And I hope that women going through these journeys continue to wake up to the spiritual nature of their sickness. The earth is calling us. We are waking up to the fact that we don't live in front of the earth as if it were a stage set. We are part of it. Its imbalances are being felt in our bodies and spirits.

When I was a girl, I had an oak tree where life felt like mine. There need to be places where children can go regularly and feel the earth as it communicates to them. That tree was my place and I was in communion with it. As a child, I didn't question that the earth was alive and that it communicated with me all the time.

That is a certain kind of knowing we can lose as we grow up. Our trees can continue to talk to us if we feel their bark, if we know what it means as their leaves change, or as the wind tells its story through the leaves.

A considerable part of my spiritual practice today is just looking and listening for a long time with the land. In my workshops, I have people spend a half hour with one square foot of land and then try some outward meditation to let go of all their thoughts except what is right there.

As we get older, we are urged to turn our concentration to reading and to make the printed pages come alive instead. We tell children, "Oh, the flowers don't talk to you. The clouds don't talk to you. The squirrels don't talk to you. This book talks to you." We've taken the mystical life out of the natural world and put it into the written word.

There certainly have been times I've sat among trees and rocks and asked a question and heard an answer. I believe birds and animals do communicate with us. Whether it's coming from the rocks, the birds or my own projection, it doesn't matter. Perhaps the important thing is trusting the answer. We tend to say, "Oh, I just made that up."

If you surround yourself with the natural world, you will find that communion. I take people out into the desert on wilderness programs and quests. I've taken people of all ages, who are very skeptical, to the desert and they come back and are certain they have had a communication with a raven or a lizard. If you quiet way down and go out for four days and nights without food or books, let yourself just be there in that place, just like when you were little and you weren't worried about time racing past, you become present to all the communion around you.

And you are walking by, and a stone catches your eye, and you go to pick it up. The first thing to remember is that it caught your attention and your whole body responded to pick it up. There is a whole dialogue going on between body and stone. I think that's conversation and that's communion.

It's important to remember this wild place isn't just a collection of rocks. This is a community of subjects evolving together. We've had this notion for 2,000 years that the world is made up of discrete substances, and that's what's real. We've ignored the reality of our interrelatedness. That is an old paradigm of the world that tells us nothing of life. Now ecologists, biologists, *physicists and other leading-edge scientists are telling us that reality is much more like a flow of energy, a flow of matter, a flow of spirit, a flow of information—all interrelated. And what once looked like discrete elements are just patterns in the flow.*

It isn't only our bodies and psyches that are sustained by these flows of energy and patterns. Our spiritual life itself depends on the richness and diversity of an interconnected world. From the beginning, the earth was a physical and spiritual reality. So the earth is trying to rebalance itself. That is what every living system does. And it's trying to do it through us.

This life then is a dance, but we only faintly hear the rhythm. We are trying to get the steps, but we've lost the music. Our own spiritual struggle can be understood as the earth's struggle to come into balance. I mean that as a quite scientific understanding of what it means to be an earthling. We are part of a larger, self-healing system. We can't help but participate.

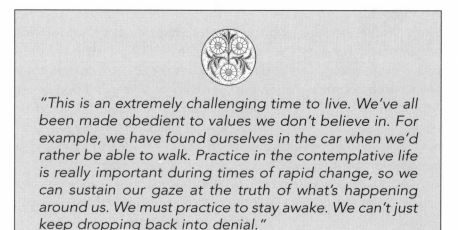

"This is an extremely challenging time to live. We've all been made obedient to values we don't believe in. For example, we have found ourselves in the car when we'd rather be able to walk. Practice in the contemplative life is really important during times of rapid change, so we can sustain our gaze at the truth of what's happening around us. We must practice to stay awake. We can't just keep dropping back into denial."

JOAN B. CAMPBELL

General Secretary, National Council
of the Churches of Christ

*"We are a nation in crisis. And that crisis, at its core,
is spiritual. I believe that the answers to our dilemma
are answers of faith and that the ecumenical vision,
if fully understood, could lead this richly textured
nation from caucus to community."*

W hen she was 16, Joan B. Campbell suffered a broken
neck in a car accident and spent eight weeks in the
hospital. But she survived—and then began to wonder if her life
was spared for a reason.

"My parents were both practical and people of faith, and
they both said, 'Maybe you are here to do something special.'
Even though that creates some pressure on you, if you are
young and begin to ask those questions of yourself in a healthy
way, it helps you make some life decisions."

The teenager from Cleveland was most certainly marked for
a special mission. From 1954 to 1967, while raising three children, she sharpened her now legendary leadership skills and
volunteered for numerous community organizations. Later, she
held executive posts with the Action for Change Program of the
Catholic Diocese, the Welfare Action Coalition, Community
United Head Start and the Action Training Network of Ohio. For
several years, she was the pastor of the Euclid Baptist Church.

Now the first ordained woman to become General Secretary
of the National Council of the Churches of Christ (NCC), Rev.
Campbell has worked for 20 years to unify churches and cultures, illuminating their common ground. Churches, she has
found, need to do as good a job as Madison Avenue at feeding
people's souls and spreading the message of harmony and

peace. "There is not much question we are an incredibly violent society right now. I have said publicly that there is a sickness in the national soul that has to be healed. I think the church, synagogue and mosque are part of the necessary ingredient for healing of the soul, but I also believe that they must heal their own divisions as well. The Scriptures say we must be one—not just for its own sake—but so the world might believe. And that is my job."

The primary impetus behind Christian unity in the United States, the NCC represents about 50 million people from Methodist, Orthodox, Presbyterian, Quaker, Baptist and other denominations. Regarded as a holistic leader and networker across cultures and churches, Campbell has also helped forge partnerships between organizations concerned with racial unity, cultural diversity, poverty, health care, the environment, education and other issues. She serves on the boards of more than 20 institutions, ranging from the Union Theological Seminary to the Christian Children's Fund. She delivers sermons and speeches to gatherings all over the world.

Her years of experience as an international spiritual leader led her to conclude that the search for the Divine is innate and timeless, Campbell says.

You think about the pioneer women who had their babies out on the trail. I don't think their search was any less than ours today. I was in Russia for Easter. To many Russians, after 70 years as an atheist society, it is remarkable to have banners on the streets in Moscow that say, "Christ is Risen." Deep in the souls of those people, through all those years, was this yearning for God, for connectedness, for spiritual strength. You look into the faces of the women, who come to the church with their faces lined and their babushkas on, and you realize they've stood there through all those years.

So I think the search for the spiritual and the Divine is eternal in people. It may ebb and flow, but probably the greatest hope our society has is that there is this yearning for spirituality. Lord knows, the violence and materialism in our society indicate we're not very close to the Divine. I think the materialism is a big piece of what is wrong because we've become dependent on things rather than the gift of the spirit. We'd share more and have less of a class society if we had more internal strength.

Reaching that core of our spirituality involves getting to that place where our mind and body are united, where our emotions and intellect have play together. That's how we find ourselves as connected human beings. I think the jobs we do tend to fragment us. People want our opinion on something or our intellectual thought on another something. Occasionally they want our feelings. It's as if everyone wants only part of you.

Your wholeness—which I think is your spiritual center—is where those things come together. The task is to be a whole person as often as possible and to bring all that you are to the tasks you are given. When you feel most satisfied with what you have done and most at peace within yourself, you have found your center.

Because I am a minister my spirituality is also my relationship to God, to a Higher Power, to a force outside of myself. All my life that relationship has been extremely important to me. My father was a surgeon and he used to say, "I feel much more comfortable taking someone into surgery when I know they have faith. Then I feel they have some relationship to wellness."

He said, "My skill alone isn't what it takes. That person must feel they can live and want to live."

So that sort of connectedness to what in my case I call God, or sometimes Jesus or the Holy Spirit, is also part of my spiritual center. People who aren't Christians refer to it in other ways. I know it's present when I feel at one or at peace with something not just inside of me, but also outside myself.

One thing that deepened my spirituality, which many women have gone through, was my divorce. I was married for 25 years and had never lived alone. I had to learn to live alone, and I found that the inner resources I had were not adequate for living alone.

I think any healthy relationship requires that you have the capacity to be alone, for that is where you develop some spiritual life.

I've had some real challenges. I've been in an emergency room all by myself and was grateful to call down a kind of spiritual strength that got me past those things. I've also had two near-death experiences. There isn't much question that those things get your attention and focus you on what's important in your life. Nine years ago, I had a heart attack and my heart stopped. I cannot claim any out-of-body experiences like the things one reads about, but the very fact that your life is perpetually put at risk or almost ended means you once again ask the questions, "What is it that is important? What is it I need to focus on in my life?" I think that is a spiritual experience. It's not just looking at your priorities. It's more looking at what really matters most.

I used to resist the idea that knowledge of self comes through suffering, but I think it does. I know that how you deal with suffering is what finally makes you an adult. Your ability to deal with suffering, problems, isolation, aloneness and all the things we fear is really what makes you into a well, psychologically sound human being. Those are the kinds of experiences that, as my grandmother used to say, "give you your mettle." I don't know of anyone who isn't touched by tragedy.

I have three grown children and five grandchildren. The experience of my heart attack made me want to spend more time in nurturing the little ones that come along and even the older ones, who don't stop needing that nurturing. So that sort of connectedness to family was renewed for me.

I am also in touch with my spiritual world when wonderful things happen. I was present when my daughter's second child was born, and I always get very teary about this. I was there when that child was born. I stood at the bottom of her bed and watched this little baby emerge. You're much too busy when your own children are being born to concentrate on them as a gift of God! But this time it hit me: "My God, this is a miracle. Here is a little person who is actually going to emerge." I can recall that today and have the same exact feeling I had when I watched it. How can people not see this as a Divine plan that is way beyond what we are capable of?

You see it in a sunset, a magnificent creation of nature. Those always make me tear up and feel closer to God. We cannot experience these things, or I personally would not like to, without God. For me it is a rootedness in faith, and it serves to deepen my faith.

I believe that the most profound belief a Christian can have is that we are absolutely interconnected. I heard Carl Sagan speak a year ago at the Cathedral of St. John the Divine. As an avowed atheist, he began his talk by saying, "As a scientist, I must say we are all connected." He spoke on St. Francis of Assisi Day, when people bring animals to the church for blessing. The message that is lifted up is the way in which earth, sky, humanity, animals and birds are all part of what I would call God's creation.

Carl and I are dear friends. My connection with this scientist and atheist is that we both deeply believe that we are connected to our environment and that what each person does ultimately impacts on the life of another. We are all interwoven in ways much more profound than we can even express. I never feel I can express this belief adequately.

When you stand in a continuum of family relationships, a mother to her daughter, a daughter to her children, those children to their children—and this is one of the gifts of being older—you see that every action we take should look to future generations. We don't live that way very often. Americans are into immediate satisfaction.

Part of our spiritual journey is to think of our spiritual connection to the past, what has been given to us and what gifts continue on. The connectedness is not just today and my lifetime but all that I have received from the past and what goes beyond me.

I think if you have a good spiritual connection, you are basically a humble person—a fairly modest person. It relieves people from the feeling that they are filled with self-importance. Your sense of worth comes more from your ability to be connected and at peace than from your external recognition from the world. We would have a better world if we had more people who didn't need so much adulation from outside themselves.

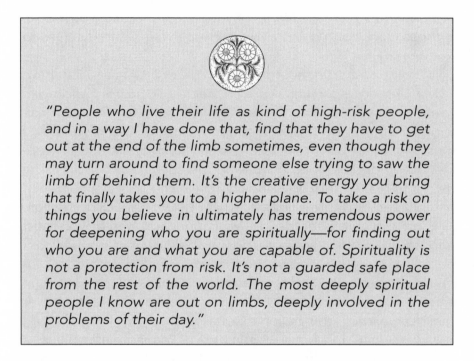

"*People who live their life as kind of high-risk people, and in a way I have done that, find that they have to get out at the end of the limb sometimes, even though they may turn around to find someone else trying to saw the limb off behind them. It's the creative energy you bring that finally takes you to a higher plane. To take a risk on things you believe in ultimately has tremendous power for deepening who you are spiritually—for finding out who you are and what you are capable of. Spirituality is not a protection from risk. It's not a guarded safe place from the rest of the world. The most deeply spiritual people I know are out on limbs, deeply involved in the problems of their day.*"

JOAN BORYSENKO

Mind-body scientist, psychologist,
author and teacher

"I think the universe has a better sense of humor than we do. It's not all so serious. It unfolds in its own delightful way, and when the intention is there for us to live a life of awareness and a life of kindness, all kinds of remarkable things begin to happen, whether or not you're following a particular spiritual discipline."

J oan Borysenko is an all-too-rare alchemy of intellect and intuition, reason and passion, pragmatism and mysticism, which explains why many regard her as a visionary for these times. One of the pioneers helping us bridge the ever-dwindling gap between medicine, psychology, spirituality and philosophy, Borysenko's vision is to bring these fields together in the service of healing.

A cell biologist, scientist, former instructor at Harvard Medical School and a licensed clinical psychologist, Borysenko cofounded and is the former director of the Mind/Body Clinic at the New England Deaconess Hospital. It was her work at the Mind/Body Clinic on which her breakthrough *New York Times* bestseller *Minding the Body, Mending the Mind* was based.

But in the past decade, Borysenko has gone beyond the science and psychology of the mind-body connection into a deeper and provocative exploration of the world's great spiritual traditions, Divine assistance, the power of prayer and miraculous healings. She states, for instance, that miracles in the form of medical healing can happen when consciousness or energy directly transform biological matter. She believes strongly that angels work to guide us daily.

Millions now embrace Borysenko's messages in her workshops, lectures and books, including *On the Wings of Light* and

Guilt Is the Teacher, Love Is the Lesson and *Fire in the Soul: A New Psychology of Spiritual Optimism.* She is a "rare jewel, respected scientist, gifted therapist and unabashed mystic," says Dr. Dean Ornish, president and director of the University of California's Preventative Medicine Research Institute. Borysenko's latest books, *Pocketful of Miracles: A Book of Daily Spiritual Practice* and *The Power of the Mind to Heal,* coauthored with her husband, Miroslav Borysenko, describe how difficult and tragic events can often bear the seeds of physical healing, transformation and spiritual awakening.

Borysenko is intimate with the kind of pain that causes growth. As a young child she was prone to mystical experiences and different states of knowing—not always pleasant ones. At the age of 10, Borysenko experienced what Joseph Campbell called a "terrifying night sea journey" that was an unforgettable rite of passage. It was 1955, and she had just moved across town. She was scared about starting at a new school, making new friends and her body's preadolescent changes. She began to experience bizarre hallucinations of poison-bearing headhunters, scorpions and snakes. And she became extremely obsessive-compulsive, washing her hands dozens of times a day and able to read only upside down and backward.

It was during this dark night of the soul that Borysenko wrote the following poem:

The Light

Somewhere in the darkest night
There always shines
A small bright light.
This light up in the heavens
shines
To help our God watch over us.
When a small child is born
The light her soul does adorn.
But when our only human eyes
Look up in the lightless skies

We always know
Even though we can't quite see
That a little light
Burns far into the night
To help Our God watch over us.

By reciting this poem over and over, Borysenko connected with the strength inside herself and found the courage to overcome her fears and compulsions.

This ability to marshal her inner self again proved invaluable in the late 1980s, when Borysenko had a successful but draining practice and research program at New England Deaconess Hospital. Overloaded and continually stressed, she drove home one night in a state of exhaustion. In one horrifying instant, she had a head-on collision. She came away from the accident relatively unhurt—except that her nose was shattered. Interpreting the collision as a "cosmic punch in the nose," Borysenko began to rediscover the importance of faith, family and friends. Once again, she discovered that crisis can be like a microscope, helping us focus in on what we truly believe.

Six months after the accident, she left her job, and she and husband Miroslav, a medical scientist, lecturer and artist, started a business that meshed their expertise in medical sciences, behavioral medicine, psychology and spiritual growth.

One of the Borysenkos' messages is that by reaching within and finding our higher selves, we can in turn reach outward in love and service to others. Joan Borysenko conducts workshops and lectures around the country for those facing life-threatening illnesses and other crises, and she also trains health care providers.

The mother of three children and one grandchild, Borysenko now lives high in the Rocky Mountains west of Boulder. Several critical factors, she believes, have spawned the spiritual resurgence sweeping the country.

We've had a chance to try on materialism and see that it hasn't made us happy. We need a certain standard of living and that's important, but beyond that, what becomes most valuable is time. Time to spend with the people you love, time to be alone, to create, to do all of those things.

Our kids are all in their 20s. They recognize that the whole economy is different now and that they will probably never make as much money as their parents. And so it makes them begin to say, "Well, if that's the case, where is happiness going to lie?" It makes this whole new generation begin to question the way they live and how they can be happy.

I think that is why we are seeing this strong interest in prayer and in creating new rituals. From the beginning of time, rituals have been a way of creating a doorway between this world and a larger reality. The glimpses we get through the doorway help us to create higher meaning in order to live more creatively and compassionately. Rituals generally open us to the Divine. We welcome the sacred mystery that acts upon us. But there is another understanding of ritual that I also like. It's called theurgic ritual, which means we're not asking God to act upon us, but we're doing something that acts upon God. In the tradition of kabbala, or mystical Judaism, theurgic rituals bring the feminine aspect of God back in union with the masculine aspect. They are a means of universal healing or repair of the world. We are in a sense co-creating with God. If we feel we're part of Divine mind, and I do, then what we do naturally affects the whole mind. If Divine mind is God, what we do in turn affects God.

From the beginning of time people have always been interested in how they can get more. And the underbelly of the New Age movement, which is like the underbelly of some prayers, is people believing, "If only I pray enough, I'll win the lottery. If only I think right, I'll manifest this red Jaguar. If only I read enough of these books about how to use the power of decreeing or the power of creative visualization, I will be able to manifest my true and perfect lover."

I think people generally end up being very disappointed with that approach. Though there's no question that when you put your mind to something you can make things happen. I have always been interested in the oldest prayers, and the most beautiful prayer of all is that of St. Francis of Assisi. It is really a prayer for selflessness: Let me look not for what I can get, but for what I can give. Let me not seek so much to be loved as to love, to be consoled as to console. And the real spiritual sense that you get from anybody who's ever immersed herself in this is that the true way to abundance and the true way to feeling loved is to give it all away. And in giving you receive.

Humility is also important in prayer. To me, humility is the essence of security, feeling that you're part of the Divine mind, which is a loving mind, and you're going to get exactly what you need. What you are trying to do in prayer is just attune yourself to that loving mind. Attune yourself by saying, "Look, let me be the best I am. Let the Godseed within me find fertile seed to grow so that whatever I'm meant to do, whatever gift it is I'm meant to share, I can do this."

And it's important to pray that way for other people, too. Because with humility also comes the sense of, "How on earth are we supposed to know what to pray for? What is the right thing?" In the case of somebody who has cancer, perhaps the right thing is that they're going to die. That's the full circle of their life. And in praying for them to live, we may be creating suffering for them or others.

It's better to pray for the best outcome to happen in that situation, whatever it is, and for all to have the strength of mind and the love in their hearts to be able to let go and let God. It's best to pray by holding in our minds a pure and holy consciousness of whatever or whomever we're praying for. This is what Spindrift, a scientific organization that studies prayer, calls nondirected prayer—as opposed to directed prayer, which specifies a desired outcome.

We each must also realize that, like prayer, a spiritual life takes different forms for different people. Perhaps what discourages people is the sense that to live a spiritual life, they're going to have to get up every morning and pray and meditate or do certain practices, and if they don't do that then they can kiss their spirituality goodbye.

I think that does a great disservice because there are people for whom that's exactly the right way to do it. They need to make their connection to God in that way. But there are other people—and I'm one of those—who connect the way that they need to.

Sometimes I'll meditate every morning. And then some-times I'll meditate here and there during the day. Some days, some weeks, I won't meditate at all. And that's the nature of what's going on. Sometimes I have great periods of journaling because something is coming up with me, and my inner life is suddenly awakened—usually during passionately difficult times.

And then there are times that I am really in tune with my dream life, and I do a lot of dream journaling. Every morning I pay attention to what I dream. Or I have periods when I do lucid dreaming. Then I have periods when I just do nothing in terms of all that. I let it lay fallow. Except I think I always have a sense of going through the day and being mindful, of being aware of my breathing.

Through the years I have accumulated a lot of little touch-stones, which have been very important for some point I was at in my life. For many years it was a medallion that I wore—actu-ally the baptismal medallion from a mystical Christian group we belonged to. I wore that for a long time, and then I didn't wear it for a long time. Then I wore it again after an AIDS patient that I'd given it to died. His family gave it back to me cast in 14-karat gold and that was very important to me.

After a while, that was superseded by an opal that I now wear, a boulder opal that I brought back from Australia. It was my gift for my 44th birthday, and it's set in the wing of an eagle. It's from a time in my life when I was really clearing out a lot of old fears. It was a very dark night, and so I wear it now all the time because that opal in the eagle wing symbolizes my rebirth.

I used to keep all of my most important touchstones in my little meditation nook. And then I realized, "Wait a minute, I spend much more time in my office than I do in that nook." So I moved all the stuff so that I could make the whole office into a sacred space. In a certain sense, if you saw my home you'd see that almost everything in it has some sort of story behind it. I feel my whole home is sacred space.

I also have a very alive relationship with the angelic realm, and that doesn't go away. That's a daily thing. But it isn't like I have to sit there for a long time. It's five minutes of tuning in and giving greetings, and then throughout the day I'm listening, and there's a give-and-take there.

My "angel practice" is based on traditional Orthodox Jewish prayers that are said before bed. After thanking God for the day, one prays for forgiveness for all errors in word, thought or deed committed in this transmigration or any other. One then extends forgiveness to others in exactly the same way. Thus purified, the Archangel Uriel is invoked before you, Michael to your right, Raphael behind you and Gabriel to your left. The shekhinah, or Divine Feminine Light of Creation, is then invoked above. I like to let the Light wash through me, revealing the same Light within my heart. I also invoke the angels throughout the day: Uriel for clarity, Michael for lovingkindness, Raphael for healing and Gabriel for strength. These attributes are the actual meanings of their Hebrew names.

That's been my particular path, but I don't expect it to be anyone else's. People approach spirituality in their own way. And you know, we really need to get over that whole concept that our spiritual life is separate from our everyday life. That our spiritual life is something that takes time or is esoteric or even requires particular practices. Because it's clear to me that real living happens in the cracks between what we consider to be the big stuff.

Spirituality really comes down to relationships with people and the ability to open your heart to other people. To have some degree of intimacy where you're welcoming that ability to give and to receive love.

And because that doesn't happen so easily, then it seems to me that spirituality is all the bumps and the bruises, the problems we have at work, the ways that our spouses piss us off and everything else. That is spirituality in action—the difficulties as well as the feelings that we go through that allow us to be *present in a different way. How can we put that off, if that's moment-by-moment living?*

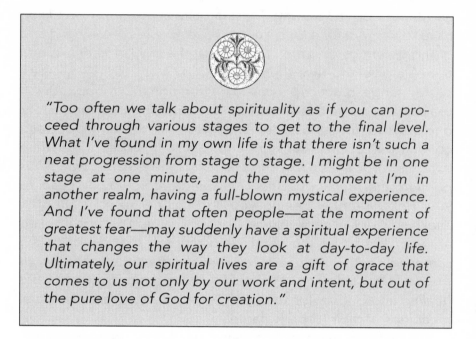

"Too often we talk about spirituality as if you can pro-ceed through various stages to get to the final level. What I've found in my own life is that there isn't such a neat progression from stage to stage. I might be in one stage at one minute, and the next moment I'm in another realm, having a full-blown mystical experience. And I've found that often people—at the moment of greatest fear—may suddenly have a spiritual experience that changes the way they look at day-to-day life. Ultimately, our spiritual lives are a gift of grace that comes to us not only by our work and intent, but out of the pure love of God for creation."

MARIAN WRIGHT EDELMAN

Founder and president, Children's
Defense Fund, and author

"I believe strongly in the gospel that says you help people who are hungry and you help people who are suffering, and you help people who need help."

Growing up in rural South Carolina, Marian Wright Edelman witnessed the philosophy of "service is the rent we pay for living" played out in her parents' lives. Her father was a Baptist minister and her mother, in addition to caring for her own five children, parented 12 foster children and ran the local "old folks' home."

Now the strongest voice for disadvantaged children in our country, Edelman keeps raising the rent she pays regularly for living. In the past 27 years, she has waged the most comprehensive and compelling campaign ever to open our eyes to the plight of our children. "It is immoral, unfair and un-American that children are the poorest group in the richest nation on earth. It is also impractical. America's quality of life, productivity and future are as inextricably intertwined with its poor as with its nonpoor children."

The organization Edelman founded in 1968, the Children's Defense Fund, educates the public about the needs of children and encourages investment in them before they get sick, drop out of school, suffer too-early pregnancies, see their families break down or get in trouble. In recent years, she has led the national effort aimed at having each child in America immunized.

Edelman first began her crusade for children in the mid-1960s after she graduated from Yale Law School and became the first Black woman admitted to the Mississippi bar. She directed the NAACP Legal Defense and Education Fund in Jackson, Mississippi, and helped save more than 100 Head Start centers from defunding. She drew national attention to the suffering of starving children in the Mississippi Delta by leading Senator Robert Kennedy on a tour of the area.

Since then, the crises faced by children have so escalated that Edelman believes they will not be solved without a massive transformation of all sectors of life, including our private and public values. How did we become so morally benumbed, she asks, that we aren't outraged by the fact that a Black child is killed by a gun every four hours? What does it say about our spiritual soul that we are not horrified by the fact that a Black child is born into poverty every 85 seconds or drops out of school every 53 seconds?

"If we do not speak, lobby, write, picket, protest and vote for these children, who will? This is not the time for despair, inaction, sulking or withdrawal. This is the time for sustained, effective and massive action to protect our children."

The crisis America faces is, at its roots, a spiritual one, Edelman says. Given that, we each have tremendous individual power to shape a better world, often beginning with the power found in collective prayer, she believes. "Gandhi reminded us that some mountains can only be moved by prayer. We need to ask God's help to overcome the mountains of family, community and moral disintegration and of escalating racial and economic polarization."

Edelman urges communities to consider weekly prayer meetings for and with children in homes and congregations. "Personal and family devotions at home and in religious congregations help our children bear the toils, snares, stresses and psychic assaults of modern life."

Ms. Edelman has won numerous awards and honors for her work, and was selected to be a MacArthur Foundation Prize Fellow. In 1990, *Ladies Home Journal* named her one of America's 50 most powerful women. She currently serves on the boards of the NAACP Legal Defense and Education Fund, the

Aetna Life and Casualty Foundation, the March of Dimes and the Robin Hood Foundation.

Edelman is the author of *Families in Peril: An Agenda for Social Change* and the acclaimed *Measure of Our Success: A Legacy to My Children and Yours*. A runaway bestseller, *Measure of Our Success* reached the *New York Times* bestseller list before its paperback release.

Edelman and her husband, Peter Edelman, who serves as counselor to the Secretary of Health and Human Services, have three sons. They live in Washington, D.C.

Ms. Edelman shares the following prayer and covenant for children, taken from her newest book, *Guide My Feet*, published in 1995 by Beacon Press:

A Prayer for Children

O God, we pray for children who woke up this morning in dens of dope rather than in homes of hope, with hunger in their bellies and hunger in their spirits, without parents or friends to care for, affirm and lovingly discipline them.

Help us to welcome them in our hearts and communities.

We pray for children who have no one to pray for them or protect and guide them and who are being abused or neglected right now by parents who themselves often were abused or neglected.

Help us to welcome them in our hearts and communities.

We pray for children who are sick from diseases we could have prevented, who are dying from guns we could have controlled, and who are killing from rage we could have averted by loving attention and positive alternatives.

Help us to welcome them in our hearts and communities.

We pray for children struggling to live to adulthood in the war zones of our cities, who plan their own funerals and fear each day will be their last. We mourn for the thousands of children whose life journeys already have ended too violently and too soon.

Help us to welcome them in our hearts and communities.

We pray for children who are born with one, two, three or more strikes already against them—too tiny to live, too sick with AIDS, too addicted to alcohol or cocaine or heroin to thrive.

Help us to welcome them in our hearts and communities.

We pray for girl children having children without hus-bands or steady friends or lifelines of support, who don't know how to parent and who need parenting them-selves. And we pray that teen and adult fathers will take more responsibility for the children they father.

Help us to welcome them in our hearts and communities.

We pray for children who are born into and grow up in poverty without a seat at America's table of plenty; for youths whose only hope for employment is drug dealing, whose only sense of belonging is gangs, whose only haven is the streets, and whose only tomorrow is prison or death.

Help us to welcome them in our hearts and communities.

We pray for children and youths in every community struggling to make sense of life, confused by adults who tell them one thing and do another; who tell them not to fight but who fight and tell them not to take drugs while taking drugs.

Help us to welcome them in our hearts and communities.

O God, we pray for children from whom we expect too little and for those from whom we expect too much; for those who have too little to live on and for those with so much they appreciate little; for children afflicted by want and for children afflicted by affluence in a society that defines them by what they have rather than by who they are—Your loving precious gift.

Help us to welcome them in our hearts and communities.

We pray for ourselves as parents, teachers, preachers and leaders, that we will help solve rather than cause the problems our children face, by struggling to be worthy of emulation, since we teach each minute by example.

O God, we pledge to pray and work to save our children's lives.

Help us.

O God, we pledge to pray and work to protect our children's dreams.

Help us.

O God, we pledge to pray and work to rekindle our children's hopes.

Help us.

O God, we pledge to pray and work to rebuild our children's families.

Help us.

O God, we pledge to pray and work to create a sense of community and security for our children.

Help us.

O God, we pledge to pray and work to instill in our children a knowledge and appreciation of their traditions and heritage.

Help us.

O God, we pledge to pray and work to leave no child behind.

Help us.

NAOMI JUDD

Entertainer, author, television
producer and mind-body lecturer

"I try to take walks in my valley and woods when I have time, and I love my animals. They keep me in touch with nature. We have to have little milestones in our days when we stop and really live in the moment and acknowledge that life is made up of these ordinary moments."

"I believe music is the breath of God. I think it's a healer," singer Naomi Judd told the audience when she and daughter Wynonna hosted their poignant farewell concert in 1991. After eight glorious years, the Judds' hard-fought road from rural Kentucky to their pinnacle as country music's most honored and successful women took a dramatic turn. Newly diagnosed with hepatitis, Naomi was often paralyzed by fear, knowing the future hung by a fine, uncertain thread.

But she called on her faith and the belief that God would reveal the next phase of her journey. Spellbound, as Wynonna sang "River of Time," Judd realized how prophetic the words she'd earlier written were: "My future isn't what it used to be, only today is all that's promised me. Flow on river of time, wash away the pain and heal my mind. Flow on river of time, carry me away."

Over the next two years, riding that river of change and transformation, Judd's life flowed on to an increasingly spiritual serenity. In two years of relative isolation on her 500-acre farm in Tennessee, she went within herself, concentrated on healing her body, intensively explored the mind/body/spirit connection and wrote her best-selling autobiography, *Love Can Build a Bridge*. Her "voyage of self-discovery and journey to wholeness" during that time of solitude helped her reaffirm that it's often the most simple things, like slowing down, that make us truly whole.

"I seem to always go back and rediscover the simple truths. I think my motto these days would be to slow down, simplify and be kind. There tends to be this headlong rush into seeing how many appointments we can cram into our calendar and how many balls we can juggle at once.

"And I am so strongly against that because until we can truly enjoy what my friend Deepak Chopra calls 'life-centered, present-moment awareness,' we are missing the whole point. The reason women are trying to rush headlong into hectic schedules is they think that will somehow make them more fulfilled or self-realized, when instead it has the opposite effect."

Judd and her husband, Larry Strickland, continue to spend much of their time on their farm, enjoying the deer, foxes, raccoons and other animals that share their land. Her daughters also have farms in the same valley. Weekends and summer vacations, she and Larry care for Casey, a 13-year-old boy they befriended in their church. And Judd stays centered by relying on her down-to-earth humor, prayer, meditation and long sabbaticals from technology. "Wy calls me a backward pioneer," Judd says. "I go for weeks without watching TV."

Judd continues to be a powerful force for love, healing and hope. Now a popular speaker around the country, she commands a different stage, sharing her experiences and life lessons. "I consider myself a communicator, because basically I'm no different from anyone else. There is nothing special or unusual about Naomi Judd. Last week, I spoke to a group of women in Tulsa, and the woman who introduced me referred to me as everywoman. I guess I kind of like that because I do feel like I am just their representative. I was a single working mom, and I've been there, done that, seen that, know it. I have held so many minimum-wage jobs," says Judd, who now tithes 10 percent of her earnings to charities.

She talks to women about their choices and the need to recognize when they can say no. Living this truth has been a surprising side effect of her illness, she says. "If I hadn't been diagnosed, I would not have learned this valuable lesson of being able to say, 'No, thank you. I've got quite enough on my plate already.'"

Through her continuing contact with the public, Judd says she senses a strong spiritual yearning. "I think our society right now is so disenchanted with materialism that there is this spiritual restlessness. Of course, that is the first insight in *The Celestine Prophecy*. When we start to feel this unsettling sense that things aren't the way they should be, that awareness is the first step.

"And the byproduct of that awareness is choice. You question, you become aware, you realize you have these choices. You have a choice to try and dress for success, have that mobile phone, fax machine and play that fast-lane game. Or you can get real honest with yourself and honor what your intuition is trying to tell you."

Trusting your intuition and faith is a practice that Judd has continuously tried to instill in her daughters, Wynonna and actress Ashley Judd. It's what she had to do more than ever before when she said good-bye to her fans to face down a life-threatening illness.

I was the happiest in my life before I was diagnosed. I had finally, for the first time in my life, obtained medical insurance and established a savings account. I actually owned my home, a concept that seemed implausibly preposterous. Wynonna and I had healed our relationship, I was putting Ashley through college and I had found my Prince Charming.

All our concerts were sellouts, the albums were platinum, the singles were number one. Could it be more perfect?

And finally all the crap that I had gone through in my life made sense because when I stood on that stage and sang I felt such a unity, such a bond with the people in that audience because I knew what it was like. I knew what went on in their homes, in their offices and in their private lives. I felt such serenity and deep fulfillment when I was on that stage because music is a transmitter. It allows direct access to each other's souls. And we could be playing at the Houston Astrodome in front of 50,000 people, which we did, and I just felt like all of us were levitating that whole building.

It was the most awesome, complete moment. So to have that so rudely taken away, not to mention the fact that Wynonna had never even remotely considered going on by herself, was indescribable. We suddenly had to perform open-heart surgery on our relationship. There were just so many layers in this crisis, but the whole time I knew God had it under control. If it hadn't been for that knowing and His peace, I would not have made it. And there were really tough times. I even began having severe panic attacks. But I knew there was a reason why I had crawled over broken glass to get there and been through all the stuff in my life.

I saw there was a reason why I was a registered nurse and a member of the mainstream medical community. And there was a reason why I was given the visibility as a singer. I just had to really free-fall into God's love and know that all of this was going to come together as a trajectory to launch me to the next phase.

I had this intuition that all of these struggles were part of the process. I knew that the stardom and the singing career weren't the grand finale. They were just part of the process. So when I felt like I was suddenly unplugged from life support—because the stage was a metaphor for life for me—I had to practice what I had been telling my children and the fans.

The other night, Wynonna, Ashley and I were sitting in a five-star hotel in Beverly Hills, and we all had on our hotel bathrobes with Pond's cold cream on our face. Wynonna was there looking for some songs for her new album, and she'd met that day with Bernie Taupin, Sammy Hagar and Sheryl Crow. Ashley had just come in from rehearsing with Robert DeNiro and Al Pacino, with whom she was doing Heat. *I had just wrapped the NBC miniseries on my life.*

So the three of us were sitting there sort of representing these different arenas of entertainment, and we all looked at each other and started talking about how I have always urged the girls to follow their intuition. Now when I look at Ashley, who is the most voracious reader I've ever known in my life, I could quote something by Rousseau about intuition.

He said, "Intuition is the sovereign intelligence which sees in the twinkling of an eye the truth in all things, in contradiction to vain and deceptive knowledge."

And Wynonna has a more direct, simple approach to things, so my personalized interpretation of intuition to her is, "Honey, that's when your gut gets it before your head gets around to figuring it out." So I was once again encouraging them to enter into projects with their intuition. We were passing around Elijah, Wynonna's six-week-old son, and I was encouraging her to follow her maternal intuition.

I am just horrified at what people must go through if they don't have the awareness that God is the Divine intelligence that runs the universe and that the universe runs on spiritual laws. My faith is what helped me succeed in my career. I credit it with why my family is healed and together. It is the reason why I have a solid, strong marriage. And it is the reason why I am alive in spite of my liver disease.

"I believe strongly in rituals. I get up every morning and have my little half-decaf, half-regular cup of coffee in my china cup and saucer. I have some wonderful instrumental tapes I listen to, and I do my devotional, whether it be reading from the Bible or something else I find intriguing. I am very blessed to have this incredible farm. This morning there were six deer standing in my yard. And at the close of the day I am in my hot bath with scented candles, and I feel a sense of timelessness."

ELISABETH KUBLER-ROSS, M.D.

Renowned death and dying expert
and author

*"These times are the darkness before the dawn.
I have high hopes for humanity, but everything is just
happening so slowly. Many more people now are at
least caring enough to look inside themselves and ask,
'What am I doing?'"*

D r. Elisabeth Kubler-Ross stumbled on some of the most profound symbols of the human spirit while visiting an abandoned Nazi concentration camp. The famous psychiatrist was terrified at the thought of seeing rooms where children stayed before they were exterminated. She dreaded seeing signs of their horror and hatred. But when she walked into one stone room, Dr. Ross was stunned to see the walls were scratched with pictures of butterflies.

"I didn't understand it, and it took another 15 to 20 years for me to really understand the symbol of the butterfly. Now it's very clear to me that our bodies are only the cocoon and our souls are the butterfly. When the time is right to die, the cocoon releases the butterfly. In the meantime, we have to learn what we came to learn, and we have to teach what we came to teach."

For almost 30 years, Dr. Ross has shared such discoveries about the resilience of the human spirit to help us all better understand how to care for the terminally ill. Internationally recognized as perhaps the foremost authority on death, dying and transition, Dr. Ross has helped health-care professionals worldwide respect and honor the needs, concerns, wisdom and fears of those facing the end of their lives. In recent years, her work has focused on the need for greater compassion and care for infants and toddlers dying of AIDS.

"I was drawn to the babies with AIDS because they are the ones who suffer the most from our homophobia and our paranoia. I wanted to adopt some of these babies when I lived in Virginia, but the people in the community were so afraid and paranoid. They would hold their breath when they drove by my farm because they thought AIDS was in the air. People are so fearful. They let their whole lives be run by fear."

Instead, AIDS should be viewed as a contemporary lesson in loving unconditionally, Dr. Ross says. "It's as simple as that. I found a gorgeous foster family near Boston that took seven of my AIDS babies, including one little girl who is now a school-aged child. When she was born, she was put in a shoebox and left to die. It was a struggle just to get her some medical help. Now this family loves her without limits. I wish the whole world could think and feel this way."

Dr. Ross's work with the dying began in the 1960s when she was assistant professor of psychiatry at the University of Chicago's Billings Hospital. Based on her work and interviews with hundreds of terminally ill patients, Dr. Ross wrote the benchmark book, *On Death and Dying*.

Published in 1969, the book was the first to identify the stages of dying, including denial and isolation, anger, bargaining, depression and acceptance. *On Death and Dying* became an instant international bestseller and is now required reading in most major medical and nursing schools, graduate schools of psychiatry and theological seminaries.

In the 1970s, Dr. Ross helped start one of the first hospices for the dying and was a founder of Children's Hospice International. In 1977 she founded *Shanti Nilaya*, which is Sanskrit for Home of Peace, in Escondido, California. The non-profit organization is dedicated to the promotion of physical, emotional, intellectual and spiritual well-being.

Until recently, Dr. Ross lived on a 250-acre farm in Virginia, a place to rejuvenate herself before going back into the world to care for others. But last year, her home was destroyed by a fire. Her favorite saying, "Should you shield the canyons from the windstorms, you would never see the beauty of their carvings," is especially meaningful as she abandons her sanctuary to begin anew in Arizona.

"At 70, everything I have collected for years is gone. I would never have left Virginia if not for the fire. But these times always turn out to be a blessing. Now I live in the middle of the Arizona desert, and the coyotes come to say good-night. I am surrounded by cactus and birds, and it's gorgeous. There is no question about it; this is a whole new beginning. I just don't know what the new beginning will be."

As in the past, Dr. Ross leans on her inner compass and faith in a Higher Power for guidance. "I couldn't have done this work without my faith. When I worked with dying patients, I knew every second, every minute that this was my job."

She concludes that the only goal in life is spiritual evolution. Blocking spiritual growth for many of us is our fixation on intellectual achievements and a feverish quest to be the best, the brightest, the most accomplished. We also must clear past emotional traumas if our spirituality is to flourish.

"You may have to go way back to your early childhood and remember and repair any traumas and memories. I believe that every human being consists of a physical, an emotional, an intellectual and a spiritual quadrant. When you resolve your unfinished business, you open up your spiritual quadrant. The idea is for all your quadrants to be in harmony. If they are in harmony and balanced, you open up like a flower."

By nurturing our spiritual natures—what she calls our spiritual quadrants—women can better understand their true calling, Dr. Ross says.

When your spiritual quadrant is opened, you become very intuitive and you follow your gut reaction. Your mind can mislead you, but your spiritual quadrant never misleads you. If you follow what you need to do, you will be on the right track. You will be on the path that you are destined to fulfill.

We have each picked our destiny before we were born. And if you can get in touch with that, it is an incredible feeling. It doesn't matter who you are, where you live or what you do. God put you here for a reason. He knows what you are meant to do. Everything happens at the right time, in the right place, in the right way—even if it's very dramatic, like my house fire. Just try to watch the "coincidences" in your life. There are no real coincidences. Not one single coincidence.

A cleaning woman in a Chicago hospital became the best teacher I had in my entire life. And she kept me going when I felt like a persona non grata. In the beginning, people hated doctors who worked with dying patients. They felt it was a waste of time and really resented us. So I had no one to talk to, and in my search for a related soul, for someone I could speak with about what was important, I noticed this cleaning woman at the hospital.

Every time I walked into the room of one of my patients, I noticed that when this woman had been there, something special had happened in that room. I can't tell you even now what that was, but it was very obvious. So finally one day, after weeks and weeks of watching this take place, I felt I had to talk to this woman and ask her what the heck she was doing with those patients.

I was very shy back then, and she was equally shy. And I didn't know that a professor of psychiatry doesn't call on a cleaning woman. But I did, and I said, "What in the world are you doing with my dying patients?" She became very defensive and backed away and said, "I am not doing anything. I am only cleaning their rooms." I said, "Wait, wait, I am not trying to stop you or criticize you." And she looked at me and ran off.

For weeks after that, we walked around each other, she trying to find out, "Who is this strange doctor?" and me trying to find out, "Who is this woman who has a gift I want to learn?" We watched each other and tried to connect silently. Finally, weeks after our first encounter, she grabbed me by my white coat and pulled me into the nurses' station.

She told me this story that made absolutely no sense to me, about how she grew up in a Black neighborhood with incredible poverty and how she'd had a three-year-old child who was very sick. She took the child to a clinic, but since she still owed them four dollars, they wouldn't admit him.

Because she had no money for the bus, she carried the child, in the middle of winter, all the way down to Cook County Hospital. She got to the hospital totally exhausted, but they kept her waiting for three hours. He died in her arms of pneumonia.

I said to her, "Why are you telling me this horrible story?" And she said, "I am not afraid of death anymore. Death is like an old acquaintance. Sometimes I walk into the rooms of these dying patients and they are so petrified of dying. I can't help but walk over to them and touch them and say, 'It's not so terrible.'"

I knew I had to learn from this woman, and I made her my first assistant in my work with dying patients. My colleagues were totally appalled and wondered, "How can this crazy doctor take a cleaning woman as her assistant?" But she taught me what no medical professor, colleague or doctor could—that it is how you feel deep down in your soul that matters, not the fancy words you use. This woman showed me this by her whole behavior and her being, not by empty words. Because of her, I didn't give up my work with dying patients.

I think our society makes spirituality harder by over-intellectualization, by thinking and thinking, instead of feeling and asking for help from those around us, as I had to do.

I recommend that people read The Quiet Mind, *by White Eagle. It's a tiny little book. If you have a question about your life or spirituality, open it up blind and you always find exactly the right spot that you need. I opened it up 100 times, and it always opened to the same place that said, "If things do not happen as you want them to happen, know that a better way is being found.*

"Trust and never forget that the true way is the way of love. Flowers do not force their way with great strife. Flowers open to perfection slowly in the spring."

And I would read this and say, "Yeah, yeah, yeah. Patience, patience, patience." For a year after, the book always opened up to the same page. I thought I had just read that page so

*much that it was turned down. So I drove three hours to this lit-
tle bookstore, got a new copy, and when I opened it—it opened
to the same page! These kinds of messages can be incredible.
They are not coincidences. That message was hammered into
me until I learned patience. It is not only thy will, it is thy time,
not my time. That is what we need to teach children. I wanted it
right now. That was my big problem.*

*Once I learned that everything happens at the right time,
then I could relax and wait. I learned that lesson when I was
about 60. If you can carry this book with you and live that way,
then you are remarkable. I have not mastered it and I am 70.
Until you die, you never stop learning.*

*"Don't drown yourself in busy work. That's not the right
thing. I raised children. I traveled thousands of miles a
year. And still I found some time for my growth.*

*"Some people find a greater spirituality through medi-
tation, some through prayer. All you need is to be still a
few minutes a day, to contemplate what you really want
to do."*

BETTY FORD

Former First Lady of the United States,
cofounder of the Betty Ford Center
and author

"I am extremely proud of the people who have found recovery through the treatment provided at the Betty Ford Center. I am also proud of the emphasis we give to the special needs of women seeking recovery."

Addressing those attending an annual reunion at the Betty Ford Center, the former First Lady said, "I don't think there is anything as wonderful in life as being able to help someone else. But believe me, it's through the grace of God that I'm able to do it."

Betty Ford's message is especially life-affirming to the more than 25,000 people who've found hope at the center because her personal battle with addiction and her bout with breast cancer once imperiled her own life.

One of the most celebrated and beloved women of our times, as First Lady, Ford charmed the public with her rare candor, spirited nature and social consciousness. She was a vocal advocate for the National Endowment for the Arts, the rights of abused and mentally challenged children, and health care for the elderly. Never one to dodge tough issues, she campaigned for passage of the Equal Rights Amendment, even when public sentiment ran against her.

As a former dance student of Martha Graham, Ford also focused much attention on the arts, particularly dance. When she and President Ford traveled to China, she visited a Chinese school and captivated the children—and the world—by dancing with them.

Then in the fall of 1974, she discovered she had breast cancer.

After her mastectomy, she went public with her illness, shattering the taboo shrouding this once intensely private disease. Her urging of other women to have their own breasts checked saved countless lives.

In 1975, the National Academy of Design named Betty Ford a Fellow, the first president's wife to receive the honor since Eleanor Roosevelt. "The most refreshing character we've had in public life for sometime," remarked renowned photographer Ansel Adams as he made the award to Mrs. Ford.

When Mrs. Ford and former President Ford left Washington, she suffered from depression and used alcohol in combination with prescription drugs for arthritis pain and sleep. "It's a miracle that combination didn't kill me," she said in a 1992 *Modern Maturity* article.

Again, Ford used her own life struggles to inspire others. At the urging of her family members, particularly then-20-year-old daughter, Susan, she received professional help to conquer her dependency. In 1982, she founded the Betty Ford Center, or Camp Betty, as it has been called, which takes a holistic approach to treatment for chemical addiction, including nutrition, physical activity, psychotherapy and spiritual renewal. At 76, Ford continues to lecture at the center regularly.

When asked to discuss her own purpose in life, Ford said, "Since I am a woman—a mother, daughter, sister and wife—it seemed quite normal to be aware of the issues that are important to women. Being able to have an impact on some of these issues and to have people listen to what I had to say has given me a sense of being a conduit for helping others through my experiences."

Today, Ford's strong sense of self is rooted in her belief in a Higher Power even in the darkest times. "We journey blind on our way back to family, to faith, to God, as we understand Him. But the blindness is a requisite part of the process. We can no longer control, we have to trust," she wrote in her moving memoir, *Betty: A Glad Awakening*, published in 1987.

Based on her own life, Ford feels that a sense of surrender and faith that God will make everything right is critical for those facing any life-threatening situation.

It gives you comfort to know there is someone or something else there working with you to overcome the crisis. Belief in a Higher Power allows you to accept that you can't do things alone. It has always helped me to remember that I am stronger when I am doing His will, not my will.

I very definitely felt the presence of a Higher Power when I was facing surgery for cancer. As I was going under the anesthesia I knew I had cancer, but I also knew I was going to conquer it.

From that moment on, I wasn't afraid. My recovery from alcohol and prescription drug dependency has brought the awareness of a Higher Power into sharper focus on a daily basis.

Today my sense of living a spiritual life, in terms of our relationships with other people, is perhaps best expressed through the Golden Rule: Do unto others as you would have them do unto you.

In our society today, we need to overcome our fear of one another, and that can only be done by reaching out and knowing the other person. The spiritual basis of the church community provides a wonderful setting for letting people relate as equals. When we are equal, there shouldn't be anything to fear.

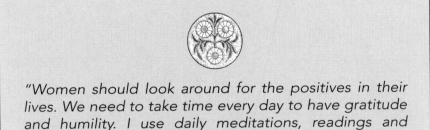

"Women should look around for the positives in their lives. We need to take time every day to have gratitude and humility. I use daily meditations, readings and prayer to keep me centered. People today feel so many pressures in everyday life. Spirituality is a calming and steadying influence that can counter those pressures."

SUSAN FORD BALES

Betty Ford Center board member
and spokesperson for Breast Cancer
Awareness Month

"My spirituality is something I don't wear on my sleeve. It's a very private and personal thing. There's something about knowing God is part of me. But I don't go around preaching about it. I just rely on it. I know it's there. And I have a lot of confidence in that knowing."

The events of our lives often seem to align to create an almost indelible map leading to our destiny. Such may be the case for Susan Ford Bales, daughter of former President Gerald Ford and Mrs. Betty Ford.

In 1974, First Lady Betty Ford had a mastectomy, becoming an overnight national symbol for breast cancer awareness. She courageously revealed her decision and urged other women to have their breasts checked, saving thousands of lives.

About 10 years later, married and raising her two young daughters, Susan Ford realized she was ready for a new challenge. Memories of her mother's brush with breast cancer were still fresh in her mind when a pharmaceutical company called and asked her to be the spokesperson for a public information campaign on breast cancer awareness. "My mom was one of the lucky ones, and thank God I still have her. So I can say to other women, 'Look, you can survive this disease. You don't have to die from breast cancer.'"

Zenaca Pharmaceuticals wanted Susan Ford as its spokesperson because breast cancer was striking younger-aged women more frequently. "My youngest daughter was two and I was looking to get back into the world again. If I'd had any idea then what this would turn into and the thousands of people I'd meet, I probably wouldn't have done it because of the time and travel involved and the time away from my family. The campaign just absolutely snowballed. We had no idea women were so wanting information and not getting it, or perhaps the messages weren't presented to them in the proper way."

Now the spokesperson for National Breast Cancer Awareness Month, it seems quite fitting that Bales carries the mantle her mother wore. "It is because of my mother's fight against breast cancer that I can relate so well to the ongoing fight against this disease." Bales is also chairperson for the Capitol Council for Early Detection, a group of wives and daughters of presidents and vice presidents who joined forces five years ago to spread the message of early detection.

Traveling up to 60,000 miles each year—typically in the fall, when her daughters and two stepsons are in school—Bales talks at medical conferences, hospital groundbreakings, women's luncheons, corporate video conferences—anything to raise the public's understanding of the disease that kills 46,000 women each year. Of special concern to her are the disadvantaged women with inadequate health care. "If a woman has to decide between spending $50 for a mammogram or to buy groceries for her kids, she's going to choose groceries for her kids. Some basic healthcare services need to be changed," says Bales, who testified before the House Subcommittee on Health and Long-Term Care about Medicare coverage for mammography screening.

Her work, though grueling at times, meshes with her parents' belief that one gives back to society, she points out. "Absolutely. When you were a congressman back in the old days, you didn't make much money. My dad got involved in politics because he truly wanted to make a difference. My mother was so open about her breast cancer then because my dad had promised America an open administration.

"I don't think my mother sat down and thought, 'I want to be a hero.' She is just not that kind of person. I don't think she ever realized the impact her openness would have, including her openness about her drug and alcohol problems. And that impact has continued for 20 years. She did what she did because that is truly what she felt was needed. And I feel that, too. I have this gene in me, too, to do the public service and work we do."

Each year when she sees what the next campaign will require of her, the schedule can seem very daunting, Bales says. But the personal rewards that flow to her create a kind of momentum that helps her touch someone anew with her message.

There is just something about being home, and there is nothing like your own bed. And you crawl into it at night and think, "Oh God, I have to get up at 5 A.M. to catch a 6:30 plane, I'll never do it." But when that alarm clock goes off the next morning, you think, "Yeah, I can. There's somebody out there who needs to hear this, and if I don't go—and I don't mean this in an egotistical way—who will deliver this message and will they get it?" And that thought just pushes you one more time in a very invigorating way.

A lot of that excitement comes down to the one-on-one interactions. There is nothing more moving than having a woman come up to me after a speech and say, "I never undressed in the light after my mastectomy until your mother went public and made it okay." Or a young girl comes and tells me she has just been diagnosed with cancer and her mother died from the disease. Or someone tells me she has just finished a chemotherapy treatment and all her hair is falling out. I run into women like these often. And they just need to be told it will be okay. There is just nothing more rewarding than seeing women who are surviving this disease and listening to their stories of survival and the traumatic experiences they've endured to continue their productive lives today.

Women need to know they can survive this disease. They don't have to die from breast cancer. And if they just practice early detection, they can detect the disease when it's very early. Fear is the biggest battle in fighting breast cancer. Fear probably kills more women than we could ever imagine. I think our psyche does more damage to us than anything. So if we can all understand breast cancer and get more comfortable talking about it, it will take some of the fear away.

Many moments, each with its own special meaning and feeling, have reaffirmed that I am doing the work I'm meant to do. Once I was the keynote speaker at a cancer hospital opening, and I watched some people leave right in the middle of my speech. It was distracting. Later when I was at the ribbon cutting, I found out that these women were oncology nurses whose mothers had died from breast cancer, and they couldn't handle my speech. They were in tears. They had become oncology nurses because they had lost their mothers. It really set me back in a way because, you know, I could have been one of those women, too. And because they were oncology nurses, they were working to change the effects of this disease.

Another time, I was part of a satellite video conference in which we encouraged Fortune 500 companies to do in-house breast cancer education and screening for their female employees. Sometimes even the copayment for a mammogram is just more than women can afford. So to listen to corporations who had offered these services to their employees describe the number of cancers they'd detected and the lives they'd saved was very special.

Another moment was receiving the Betty Ford Award from my mom and dad, which was a real special thing, to have your mother get up and say, "Thank you for doing this. Thank you for taking this work over and being such a crusader." It's just so special listening to your mother describe how wonderful you are. I said, "You did raise me, I do believe."

There's something about being role models and being put on pedestals that I hated when I was in the White House. I know I am making an impact, but I guess I don't like to think of myself in a leadership role. I am more such a normal person, whatever that means. I cook, I garden, I raise money for the PTA.

I just want people to say, "She made a difference. She helped us raise money. She helped make the contact for a donation. She was the chairwoman. She was involved." If I put my name on something, I will be involved and be a part of it.

"Finding balance in your life is really important, and everyone's threshold is different. I don't think I could do the work I do at the pace I follow for 12 months a year. I would literally run out of energy and my family would disown me! My balance is to go hard for three months, and then I am home. I get rejuvenated and reconnected with the house, family and school. I know when I go at it full tilt, I get in trouble. And when I sit back and reflect, 'Do I really approve of this?,' I don't. If you don't take time to reflect about your life, the repercussions are just brutal. You lose track of things and nothing has meaning. I guess the biggest thing is learning how to say, 'No. I would love to do that, but I just can't.'"

JANE GOODALL

Scientist and founder of the Jane
Goodall Institute, and author

*"A sense of wonder is desperately important. Wonder
and being able to laugh at ourselves and realizing how
terribly arrogant we have become because of a mistaken
belief that man has dominion over the birds of the air
and the fish of the seas. The word 'dominion' was
actually a translation of the Hebrew word 'stewardship.'"*

Possibly the greatest gift we can give our children is to
instill in them a sense of awe and wonder and respect for
all living creatures, says renowned scientist and humanitarian
Jane Goodall. For if they can show concern for the smallest
moth, then surely they will respect one another more.

In 1960, the 23-year-old Goodall, having saved up her fare by
working as a waitress in England, arrived on the shores of Lake
Tanganyika in northern Tanzania. She was at last living out her life-
long dream to study animals in the forest. "I can't remember a time
when I didn't long to go to Africa to study animals," she once wrote.

The young woman could hardly have known, as she slipped
into the African rain forest to spy her first chimpanzee, that she
would conduct the longest continuous field study of any living
creature and, in the process, completely revolutionize thought
about the animal kingdom and human evolution.

But Goodall's mother, Vanne Goodall, guessed early on that
her daughter had a unique destiny. The girl who loved Tarzan
and Dr. Doolittle was once caught in bed watching earthworms
as they moved around her pillow. Another time, after searching
for six hours, her mother reported Goodall missing to the
police. She then found her curious daughter bursting with
excitement because she'd just spent five hours in the hen
house—waiting patiently for a hen to lay her egg.

"My mother was the one who most inspired me. When I dreamed as a child of going to Africa, her friends said, 'Tell Jane to dream about something she can achieve'—because Africa was known as 'the dark continent' in those days, and young ladies didn't go tramping off into the forest. Moreover, we didn't have any money.

"But Mum used to say, 'Jane, if you really want something, and you work hard enough, take advantage of opportunities and never give up, you will find a way.' My family has always been immensely supportive of me, and I would say that is a very key ingredient in what I am now."

Goodall has spent the past 35 years continuously studying, and often living with, the same community of chimpanzees in an area of Tanzania now known as Gombe National Park. Atop a clearing about 1,000 feet above Lake Tanganyika, which she called "the Peak," Goodall gathered the world's first view of their nature in the wild. She eventually discovered that chimpanzees have behavioral patterns, cognitive abilities and emotions remarkably similar to those of human beings. She was amazed to see them embrace, kiss, hold hands and pat one another on the back.

She sent shock waves through the scientific community when she observed wild chimpanzees using and even making tools—a skill previously believed to separate man from other animals. In 1977, one of Goodall's supporters created the Jane Goodall Institute for Wildlife Research, Education and Conservation, now based in Ridgefield, Connecticut, with offices in Canada, the United Kingdom, Tanzania, Germany, Burundi, the Congo and Uganda. The author of six books and countless articles, and the recipient of prestigious awards—ranging from the National Geographic Society's Hubbard Medal to the Kyoto Prize in Basic Science, the Japanese equivalent of the Nobel Prize—Goodall says her philosophy of life embraces the idea that the spiritual is very important.

"The 'spiritual' being a sense of at-oneness with nature, a knowledge of purpose, of being part of a master plan, in which we have the option of taking advantage of the opportunities laid before us. I suppose, coming to the heart of it, my belief in a spiritual power provides purpose and strength to my life—the key word being strength."

Her own spirituality first flourished in the Congregational Church when she fell platonically in love with the parson. "I then became intensely spiritual and felt we were united by a spiritual bond," she laughs. "It was, in fact, nothing but an adolescent crush on someone but it opened up a doorway to a different sort of world from that which I'd known as a schoolgirl. It made me think about a lot of things that are not talked about much every day, such as our relationship with a spiritual power."

As her late husband was dying of cancer, Goodall felt no belief in any God at all. Soon, however, she was convinced by experiences after his death that there is, indeed, a state of being-ness that doesn't end at death. "My belief in a power underlying the emergence of life on earth, and the reality of spirit, was rekindled."

Today, instilling in children around the world a sense of wonder in and respect for all plants and creatures is her "highest priority." Her newest mission is a program called Roots & Shoots, which helps children value themselves, each other and all living things while becoming actively involved in environmental and humanitarian issues. Roots & Shoots kids in more than 20 countries are planting trees, leading community recycling programs, creating organic gardens, putting up bird houses, visiting children in the hospital, studying environmental problems and sharing problems and solutions with students in other countries.

"Children are not born with a defined set of moral values. They need clearly explained rules to enable them to adjust and contribute to the society into which they have been catapulted."

As Goodall knows better than anyone today, children's instincts for compassion, self-sacrifice and love are rooted in their primate heritage. Sadly, so, too, are the instincts for cruelty and anger.

I think Roots & Shoots is probably the reason I came into the world. Yet I couldn't have done it without all those years with the chimpanzees and an understanding that led to a blurring of the line between "man" and "beasts." The chimpanzees taught us that after all, we humans aren't as unique, compared with the rest of the animal kingdom, as we used to think.

This led to a new awareness—a new respect—for the other amazing non-human beings sharing our planet. The trouble is, this awareness caused us to admit to ourselves that we humans aren't the only beings with personalities, aren't the only beings capable of rational thought, aren't the only beings capable of emotions like joy and sorrow and fear and despair, or the only beings capable of mental or physical suffering. This realization raises tough ethical issues when we start to think about the ways in which we use and abuse non-human animals in so many ways in our daily lives.

These are issues that everyone must face for themselves. Only if children grow up with respect for all living things will the planet have a chance for survival. I don't side with the environmentalists who believe the planet is doomed. I believe we have hope because I have great faith in our ingenuity. Our extraordinary intellects enabled us to develop increasingly sophisticated technology, much of which led to an enormous amount of good. Unfortunately, destructive by-products, as well. That, along with our capacity to overreproduce ourselves, has created a very dire situation. But I firmly believe that now that we understand the problems, we can start to work together to heal some of the wounds, using those same amazing intellects.

But we have to make changes in our behavior and attitudes. Waste, to me, is one of the awful crimes of our society. We in the developed world live in a consumer society. After years in Tanzania, it really hurts me to see the horrendous waste in the States and the UK. We are greedy. We are raping the planet's resources. We take products from Africa and the developing world and bring them over here, and we waste them. If only families would start thinking more about what they need and what they do with what they don't need. I know most households use far too much electricity and water and buy more food than they really need. That is one important area every family can work together on.

Children give me particular hope because they have more open minds. They aren't as set in their ways. It may be easier for them to understand the hardest message of all. The message that even in a typical day, just about all of us in the Western world do something we know perfectly well isn't environmentally sound.

Like throwing out batteries even though we know the acid from them will eventually leak out and pollute the ground. We think, "Well, there are millions and millions of people, and that is one tiny battery, and what I do can't possibly make that much difference. I am one tiny person."

We must learn to think with a different perspective, for there are millions of people around the earth with the same "just me" syndrome. Kids seem to understand this better than a lot of adults. Often they come up all excited after a talk and say, "I'm going to tell everyone what you said about the battery."

There is a tremendous amount of idealism in children, but they need heroes and heroines. Around the world there are truly amazing and incredible people just shining out with the power of the human spirit. People who have overcome tremendous difficulties and still carry on. Roots & Shoots programs will create opportunities for children to meet some of these people. It is also important that children have contact with animals and experience nature. Even if they only have plants in the classroom, they have something green and growing.

Nature, for me, is the most powerful medium for experiencing spiritual power. Or when I go into an old cathedral where I can feel a sense of the past that will continue into the future.

There really are strong environmental and spiritual movements afoot, and there's no question attitudes are changing as around the world people become aware of the problems we face. But often it seems that something is needed to take this new awareness one stage further—to get it past just talking, realizing and understanding into commitment and action. I would like to see Roots & Shoots spread into different countries around the world. It would be so wonderful if everyone grew up understanding how arrogant we've been in our assumption that the planet was created for us alone. I want children to understand that every life—human and non-human—has meaning and value.

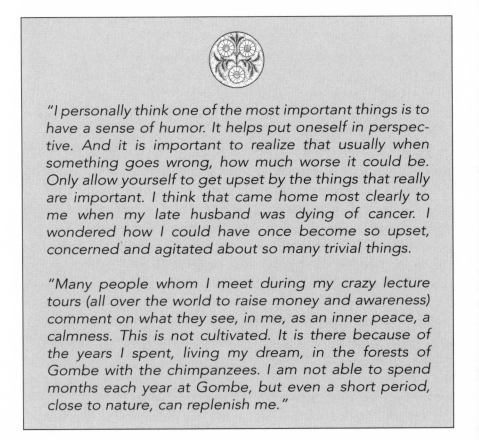

"I personally think one of the most important things is to have a sense of humor. It helps put oneself in perspective. And it is important to realize that usually when something goes wrong, how much worse it could be. Only allow yourself to get upset by the things that really are important. I think that came home most clearly to me when my late husband was dying of cancer. I wondered how I could have once become so upset, concerned and agitated about so many trivial things.

"Many people whom I meet during my crazy lecture tours (all over the world to raise money and awareness) comment on what they see, in me, as an inner peace, a calmness. This is not cultivated. It is there because of the years I spent, living my dream, in the forests of Gombe with the chimpanzees. I am not able to spend months each year at Gombe, but even a short period, close to nature, can replenish me."

CHRISTIANE NORTHRUP, M.D.

Holistic gynecologist, founder of
Women to Women, and author

"When I teach medical students, I tell them, 'Like it or not, the shaman's cloak is on your shoulders. What you say has great power to either heal or not heal. At the same time, you are not all powerful. If you don't believe in a power greater than yourself, you will have a terrible, lousy career. But if you allow yourself to be a channel for something greater, then you and your patients can have a healing partnership that's really fun.'"

We wander far afield for happiness these days, sampling sunrise yoga, Zen retreats or shopping binges only to often find the answers we seek as close as our own breath. Because our bodies constantly strive to wellness and wholeness, they are often the best yardstick of our physical, mental, emotional and spiritual health, says Dr. Christiane Northrup.

A holistic gynecologist and surgeon, Dr. Northrup is fast gaining an international reputation for her ability to mesh modern medicine with ancient beliefs and treatments, such as diet, herbs, recognition of the body's energy chakras and the power of thoughts to heal.

She has helped countless women at last find medical relief by tracing the psychological or spiritual roots of their illnesses. What conventional medicine fails to recognize, says Dr. Northrup, is that many physical illnesses, from fibroid tumors to breast cancer and endometriosis, often begin as blocked emotions. "You have to understand that in the 17th century, Descartes cut a deal with the Roman Catholic Church that said, 'Okay, doctors get the body and priests get the soul.' So all of our line of reasoning has been to take the soul out of the body. Split these two parts, rend them asunder and our alienation from our bodies and nature is the result."

Dr. Northrup weaves a great deal of her personal embroidery into the fabric of her medical practice, which is grounded in the mind, body and spirit connection. In 1981, her medical degree secured from Dartmouth, she was part of a demanding, male-dominated OB/GYN practice. While working 80-hour weeks, she also cared for and nursed her newborn daughter. And then she developed a severe breast infection. Instead of nurturing her own body and spirit—she had to prove she could pull her own weight—she maintained her pace. "As a good daughter of the patriarchy, I worshiped at the altar of efficiency and productivity."

Soon, her body's cry was thunderous. Feverish, delirious and shaking with chills, Dr. Northrup went to the hospital and discovered that the infection had spread so dramatically it had created an abscess deep in her breast that penetrated into her chest wall.

Two years later, when she tried to nurse her second daughter, she found the breast would give no milk. The gods, Carl Jung once wrote, visit us through illness. It was time to revisit and recreate her life, Dr. Northrup concluded.

In 1986, she started Women to Women, a health center in Yarmouth, Maine, devoted strictly to women's health issues. She continues to see the vibrant improvements that occur in women's lives when they learn how to better respect and care for themselves. Many of Dr. Northrup's relationships with her patients are captured in her pioneering 1994 book, *Women's Bodies, Women's Wisdom: Creating Emotional and Physical Health and Healing.*

"I ask women to ask themselves, 'What would it be like if you reclaimed the wisdom of your body and learned to trust its messages? What would your life be like if you no longer lived in fear of germs or cancer? How would your life be different if your body were your friend and ally? How would your life be different if you learned how to respect your body as though it were a precious creation—as valuable as a beloved friend or child?'"

She often counsels patients who must reshape their lives, as she did hers, to fully express their creativity. When women reach that juncture in their life's path and yearn to make a change, Dr.

Northrup offers the following advice: "One of the first things you do—and this is really, really true—is you go outside and say to your angels, 'Tell me my next step. Give me a sign. I am ready to know what is the best, highest and most fun use of my life.'

"Then stand back for the roller-coaster ride because the first thing that may happen is you might get fired from your job. Don't do this unless you really want to know. Don't mess around with spiritual guidance because this is key: The degree to which you get sick in your life is the degree to which what you say you believe and how you live your life differ from each other. You can't say you want Spirit to guide your life and then stay in a marriage when you are being asked to leave, or stay in a job that is killing you when your whole guidance system is telling you otherwise."

Dr. Northrup's own inner guidance system and ability to celebrate the mind, body and spirit synthesis was first nurtured by her family's philosophies and experiences with life—and with death.

It all started with the family I grew up in. We were called a health-nut family. My dad was a dentist, and he would be considered a holistic dentist now. He thought you could see someone's health by looking in their mouth. His brother and sister were medical doctors who followed the standard conventional model, but 30 years ago, we were the ones grinding wheat flour, eating organic beef, making yogurt and jogging. Of course, we also ate a lot of apple pie and ice cream! But we had a sense of our connection with nature, and that it and the soil our food came from counted.

I also had some powerful experiences growing up. I had a sister die in the hospital when she was three months old. She was born and wouldn't eat, and the doctors didn't know why. They kept her hospitalized. My mother could not hold or feed her, which is what they did then, and she died in a pool of vomit. My mother felt it was an awful experience—to just look at your child through a glass window and not be able to do anything.

The next child born, my brother, also wouldn't eat for unknown reasons. And remember, we were a medical family and we still couldn't figure out the problem. This time, my mother signed out my brother against medical advice. The doctors said, "If you do that, he will die." But she knew that if she left him at the hospital, he would die. The doctors had also said my brother was retarded because he held his hands in a funny way when he cried. My mother said she knew he wasn't retarded, and she knew the doctors didn't know what was going on. If my parents hadn't trusted themselves, my brother would be dead. He is alive and well today.

Another time, when I was interviewing for my internship, my dad signed himself out of an intensive care unit where he'd been taken because of chest pains. He called and said, "Come and get me, the doctors don't know what is going on with me." When he got home he had fluid two-thirds of the way up in his lungs—he actually had an inflammation in the sack around his heart—but he just sat in a chair until he got better. If the doctors had simply talked to him and said they didn't know what was going on, he could have trusted them.

So I had some key experiences of appreciating medicine because I had it all around me. I appreciated the good stuff and I also knew medicine wasn't a god. It couldn't save people. Sooner or later, you had to trust your own gut instincts about what was going on.

I had to do that in my own life after I developed a fibroid tumor when I was writing my book. Fibroid tumors are usually related to creativity that hasn't been birthed yet. But only the woman herself can ultimately decide what they're about. Dietary factors are also involved. Forty percent of women in the United States have them, which is not surprising. When my tumor developed, I drew a tarot card from the Mother Peace Divination Deck, which I use as a personal divination system. I love it. I asked, "What is the highest purpose served by my fibroid? What is it trying to teach me?" And I drew the devil card, which showed someone on top of a hierarchical pyramid chained to people below him. It represents the domination of the intellect over everything else and being chained to forms that no longer serve.

I saw that the form I was chained to was my association with Women to Women and my continuing to see patients in the old way. Though I had changed my practice dramatically from the 1980s—it isn't even comparable to conventional OB/GYN—it still required another change. It's like unpeeling the layers of an onion. You peel one layer off, and then you peel another, and then you get to what your beliefs are now.

With Women to Women, my belief was that, "No one can do medicine the way I do it. Therefore I have to do it because if I don't do it, no one else will." So that was another belief system I had to peel away.

What my fibroid has done for me is to show me, "Okay, are you really going to put your money where your mouth is? If you truly believe you constantly need to update your life and stay in the flow of creativity, then even something as great as Women to Women needs to change."

On a higher soul level, my fibroid was really a manifestation of a lesson I learned from my body, a lesson that is so indigenous to all of us. The beauty of having a fibroid I can feel on my abdomen is that I know when it is big and when it is small. And I have learned more from this thing than you can possibly imagine. Now I am slowing my energy, my thoughts, my emotions, and seeing how the fibroid changes. And then teaching others what I learn.

As I finished the manuscript for my book, the fibroid shrank a lot. Currently, I find when I am excited about my life and I am exercising and I am very clear about my creative ideas, in one day, the fibroid can shrink in half. What Einstein said is indeed true— $E = mc^2$—matter and energy are completely interconvertible.

Now I realize my fibroid was absolutely trying to tell me it was time for a change. That's why I have decided to stop seeing patients at the office. It is not the best use of my energy anymore. There's a way of educating people and changing the culture that you cannot do when you're seeing 15 individual patients a day— and that's taking all your energy. The closer you get to your life's work, the fewer trade-offs and sacrifices you can make.

Everywhere I go, women are wanting more practical, usable, grounded information about their health. Now I reach many more people through my newsletter, through videotapes and audiotapes, and by teaching women, physicians and medical students.

Women to Women will continue to be as strong as ever. My colleagues and two nurse practitioners have very viable, wonderful practices. New women practitioners will most likely continue to join us. I will remain a part of Women to Women but in a different role. Also, as I've traveled around the United States and abroad, I've met many like-minded women health-care practitioners who are starting centers like Women to Women. So Women to Women is no longer limited to Yarmouth, Maine. It is happening globally.

It's lovely to make a change when I don't have a crisis, when I have so many choices. But no matter what you choose, you always have to take a leap of faith, with no guarantees.

We all have to be willing to recreate ourselves regularly. And we know from nature that when something new is born, something old has to die. How do we know what our next step should be? Always go with the thing that makes you feel the best on all levels and brings you the most enthusiasm and excitement. Feel your way through life instead of thinking your way through life. You will always know when you are creating in your life because it will be accompanied by enormous enthusiasm and by enormous terror at the same time.

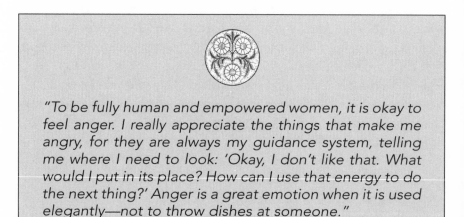

"To be fully human and empowered women, it is okay to feel anger. I really appreciate the things that make me angry, for they are always my guidance system, telling me where I need to look: 'Okay, I don't like that. What would I put in its place? How can I use that energy to do the next thing?' Anger is a great emotion when it is used elegantly—not to throw dishes at someone."

SOPHY BURNHAM

Journalist, playwright and author

"I don't doubt for one moment the incredible importance of adoring springtime when it comes and of loving one another. Our purpose is to love one another, to love those around us, to love ourselves. Love, love, love."

"I have seen the truth," Dostoyevsky said. "It is not as though I had invented it with my mind. I have seen it, *seen it*, and the living image of it has filled my soul forever."

Since the beginning of time, men and women have expressed such rapturous celebrations of their wholeness. By reading the revelations of Dante, Socrates, Emily Dickinson, St. Francis of Assisi, Albert Einstein, Hildegard of Bingen and so many other "souljourners," we find meaning in our own experiences of God.

As we approach the next millennium, many of us find such sustenance from the words of Sophy Burnham. One of our most eloquent contemporary chroniclers of how the Divine is revealed, Burnham says the quest for greater spiritual meaning is universal. "If you scratch the people of any culture, there has always been a search for God. We are composed of a Divine spark, and we long for that Divine unity. We long for it in our country-and-western songs, in our celebrations of spring, and we long for it in our suffering."

An accomplished novelist, journalist, nonfiction writer and playwright, Burnham catapulted to international visibility in 1990 when her book, *A Book of Angels* was published. Initially, she never intended the book for publication. She said she only wanted to gather the magical, mysterious, implausible things that had happened in her life and turn the stories like stones in her hand and see what sense they made.

Her own visits from angels were some of the captivating moments she sought to understand. One such angel appeared, not in winged beatitude, but in the form of a swan. One cold autumn night "with a three-quarter moon climbing through the milk of stormy clouds," Burnham and her husband went sailing on Long Island Sound. After finding a calm spot to anchor the boat for the night, they woke at midnight to find themselves drifting offshore in the dark, the anchor line snagged on the propeller, the anchor pulled free. After they pulled the remaining anchor line taut, a white swan suddenly appeared.

After Burnham cast some bread on the water, the swan had to swim backward as fast as it could against the current to reach it. "Oh swan," Burnham said, "I wish that you could dive underwater and release the anchor rope." As the swan stared at her, her husband shouted, "It's free! It's free!" The next morning, when Burnham searched for a family of swans on the marsh, there were none.

To have such an encounter with the Divine is like "standing on a hillside at night, in the midst of a thunderstorm," Burnham wrote in *A Book of Angels*. "All around lies darkness and rolling black clouds, and suddenly the sky is torn open by a sheet of lightning and there exposed before you is the whole valley, trees, pastures, woods, streams, hills. The lightning ends, you are plunged again into darkness. But now you know what's there, and no one in the world can persuade you that you imagined what you saw."

After a mystical encounter, you do everything as you once did, yet you sense life in profoundly different ways, she explains. Our joys are more acute, and our ability to sense others' suffering is keener.

After one mystical experience, Burnham discovered, almost accidentally, that she had the power to heal. She has participated in healing services at the National Cathedral in Washington, D.C., in which priests and lay people join together and lay hands on parishioners to send them the light of God.

"The services are absolutely beautiful. Just beautiful. Each of us has some healing capacity. I came down from my mystical revelation and saw this light shining off my hands, and all of a sudden I had healing power. Soon after that I was directed almost by accident to this class on healing. Yet every mother who picks up her baby and kisses him when he falls down and scrapes his knee, gives a healing kiss. It is the touch of love. It is the touch of compassion."

A Book of Angels was fiery kindling for the public's passion for celestial concerns. It has sold more than 1 million copies, and Burnham went on to publish three more books on angels and their mysterious and miraculous work. Currently the executive director of the Fund for New American Plays, she has two grown daughters.

Burnham is now writing a book about mystical experiences. One conclusion she has reached is this: As dramatic as a brush with the Divine can be, it is not that luminous moment that matters, but how you live the remainder of your days.

Mystical experiences are dramatic, fantastic, and they carry us to new levels. But in and of themselves the visions are unimportant. It is what happens afterward that is important. They change your whole life. Your whole life turns around. A true mystical experience transforms you, but the experience itself is much less important than how it affects you.

Was it truly a mystical experience? Well, if so, it will be evidenced in the way you lead the rest of your life. Because you won't be the same.

I meditate every day and sometimes my meditations are full of fantastic light and union, and sometimes they're not. And it doesn't matter. Light, dark, something, nothingness. Now I understand it's all the same. Because there isn't any one dramatic moment of a Higher Power evidenced in my life. The spiritual is happening all the time, as insight, nudging, knowledge.

Just a recent miniscule example: I needed to talk to someone, but I couldn't just call her up and say what I wanted to say. Weeks passed. One day, I needed to go to the market. I thought, "I have no food in the house. God, I hate to go to the market."

All of a sudden this inner sense said, "Go right now to S——," which I don't usually go to. And I asked myself, "Why go there?" and the answer came back, "Because she is there right now." And I went, and she was indeed there. We stood together at the checkout counter and I said the words I needed to say to her, and she went off. And I hope our relationship is the better for it. Time will tell.

That kind of thing happens so frequently that it's no longer anything unusual. These gifts are given to us all the time. These events happen to everyone. Some people discount it. They say it's luck or coincidence or that "they" did it. It's that kind of hubris.

But most people, by the time they get to their middle years, particularly if they have had any kind of brush with danger or death, develop that joyful sense that we are not really in control. It's a terrifying recognition at first, and then you understand the partnership and the relief.

But it isn't a relief at first. It's scary. It may ask a lot of you. But the help is always there, too. It's no longer that horrible scraping on gravel you get when you are doing it all by yourself or you forget to ask for the highest good. I use the image for myself of being on a road in the dark, blindfolded. I am walking down this road and sometimes I come to the gravel on the shoulder. Now—these days—I need just the finest little silken neck rein to pull me back. But I used to need to stumble on the shoulder and have an electric cattle prod push me back to the middle of the road.

And I would be so stunned by it that I would stumble over to the far side and get prodded on that side. It took me a long time to get sensitive to the messages so I could walk in the right path.

As you evolve spiritually, you also become more sensitive and possibly more touched not only by your own suffering, which you can name, but by that of others and the compassion you feel for them. We feel pain and experience suffering so we can extend the cup of kindness to one another. If there was no pain, what would you do? How would you care for one another? How would you love one another? We don't love only in pain, but we find our humanity in this suffering.

Once I was in a period of most intense emotional pain, and went for a walk up this hill near my house toward the woods. I could barely move. I was doubled over, holding my gut; every cell in my body hurt, and I couldn't stand up straight. I felt I had a great yoke on my shoulders. I hurt so much that as I was walking up the hill, it suddenly occurred to me, "Christ must have walked like this." And then I thought, "I am so willing to take the love of God's gifts, why would I not take the fire of His love as well!" And then, "If this is the gift of the love of God, I can take more—much more. Give me a thousand times more pain than this!" The minute I opened to it, the pain was gone. And never returned. I have to remember that. If I can remember that every single thing comes from God, if I can place myself utterly in the hands of the Master, accepting whatever happens with an open heart, then everything works out right. When I try to force my will, then everything turns out wrong.

But there's a balance. I don't mean I give up. I surrender. I work at things. I don't abdicate responsibility.

I believe that we each come here to our lives with a purpose. From a very early age, I have had a sense of what my purpose is, although it also has shifted at different periods of my life, deepened and taken on shadings with the years. Right now my purpose is to try to live each moment so alertly, with such clarity and with such love and compassion, that I am aware both of this physical world in which we live—this material daily world of people, work, children, cars, food, skies and meadows, skyscrapers and subways, homeless and wealthy—and simultaneously see each moment as spiritual, too.

From the time I was very little, I thought, "I am going to be famous one day." It was both a frightening and an exhilarating idea. So then I would think, "Well, everyone has that feeling. It is just a childhood idea." But I also knew I was supposed to write something. I didn't necessarily know what I was going to write. I remember sitting at a pool with my children when they were very young and thinking, "I can't stand it. I ought to be home working. I am not living my purpose and there is not much time." You have to listen to that. It is really hard if you have a true calling. You have to heed that calling.

Until fairly recently, there was something that wasn't right, that wasn't fulfilled. Once I finished my series of books, I said, "There, I have done what I was supposed to do." I am only halfway through my life. Obviously there is a lot more!

Whether or not my work touches anyone is not in my control. What I think I did was to come here to this plane, saying, "Okay, this time I will be a writer. And I will try to write some things I know." Whether anyone reads them is not the point. There is an ego that would love my work to be known throughout the world and to move people to higher realms and all that. But that's actually in God's hands and not Sophy's. All she could do was try with all her heart and mind and soul as hard as possible. It might be that none of it worked out. There can be little accidents that throw you off course. But the point was to try.

"I've said three prayers in my life. When I was a child, I said, 'I want to be beautiful,' because I thought only beautiful women had power. Then I said, 'I want to be a boy,' because I thought boys had power. And then I said, 'I want to understand,' and that was my prayer for many years. Now I have other prayers besides."

TERRY TEMPEST WILLIAMS

Naturalist writer and
environmental activist

"It is all about what we know in our bodies, what we know in our hearts. Until we start looking at the land as our own bodies, until we start looking at our bodies as landscape, no separation, seeing them whole, even holy, I don't know how we can step forward in compassion."

atural beauty has a necessary place in the spiritual development of any individual or society, wrote Rachel Carson in the 1960s. "I believe that whenever we destroy beauty, or whenever we substitute something man-made and artificial for a natural feature of the earth, we have retarded some part of man's spiritual growth."

Thirty years later, we have, blessedly, other women's voices to coax us into fully seeing our spiritual and physical connectedness with all living things. Naturalist writer Terry Tempest Williams' poetic, passionate descriptions of her love of landscape are among the most sensual and sacred odes to our collective need for wild hearts and wild places. Her books include *Pieces of White Shell: A Journey to Navajoland, Coyote's Canyon, Refuge: An Unnatural History of Family and Place, An Unspoken Hunger* and most recently, *Desert Quartet.*

"Each of the books I've written is spiritual at core. For me, there is no separation between a spiritual life, a secular life, a life engaged. It is seeing the world whole, even holy.

"From my point of view, being in nature, being in a landscape or being in the heart of wildness reminds us of who we are and what we are connected to."

Williams' physical tie to the land and how that bond runs through the threads of her own family is lovingly and rawly chronicled in *Refuge*. The book captures the devastation to the Bear River Migratory Bird Refuge as the Great Salt Lake rises in 1983 and threatens the waterfowl and shorebirds Williams has always lived with and drawn strength from. "It is a matter of rootedness, of living inside a place for so long that the mind and imagination fuse," she writes.

As the lake rises, Williams' mother also notes a rise in her abdomen. She is diagnosed with ovarian cancer. Her mother, Williams shares, was exposed to radioactive fallout from routine atomic bomb tests in Utah in the 1950s. Williams, too, remembers in a dream, sitting on the lap of her pregnant mother, watching an aboveground atomic bomb test.

"In writing *Refuge*, certainly the question that burned deeply was, 'How do we find refuge in change?' Suddenly I found myself in the midst of deep change, up to my ankles in the rising Salt Lake and with a heart that was breaking over my mother's diagnosis with cancer."

Williams kept a journal and, as a naturalist, recorded the lake's rise. As a daughter, she chronicled her family's struggle with her mother's illness and eventual death. When she reviewed the writings, she realized the lake's levels corresponded exactly to her family's emotional levels. "What I saw once again was no separation between our lives and nature. Two seemingly disparate stories were, in fact, the same thing. I find that fascinating and extremely encouraging. We are not alone in the processes of life."

Throughout her mother's illness and after her death, Williams found a "stability of soul" from times of solitude in nature, whether with the birds or in the canyon country of southern Utah. "The solitude in nature is the solitude I carry within me at my core. I believe the hours one spends in the land ultimately become a reservoir within one's soul."

It was her great-grandmother, Vilate Romney—who came to Utah with her husband and daughter from Mexico—who first instilled in Williams the sense of drawing on her inner stability for outer change. "Almost every time I was with her she would say, 'Faith without works is dead.' I think there is a great tendency among us to say, 'Well, I am doing the inner work.' And that's really important. I strongly believe in meditative practices and keeping that core solid. But I also think a spiritual life requires outer work. The two are simultaneous."

Transformation in our society will come through individual suffering and reflection—but also through extremely hard work, Williams says. "I think that demands a depth of personal commitment, the making of vows. We must ask ourselves the question, 'What are we willing to give our life to? What are we committed to? What are we willing to sacrifice for?'"

Her sense of environmental activism—her "sacred rage"— has taken Williams to Congress, to testify against clear-cutting practices that threatened the Pacific yew trees used to treat cancer, and to hearings in her own state on wilderness designation. *Newsweek* identified Williams as someone likely to make "a considerable impact on the political, economic and environmental issues facing western states in this decade." *UTNE Reader* named her one of *UTNE*'s "100 who could change your life." Williams' own activism and love of land, along with that of other visionary women, such as Rachel Carson, calls forth from her most recent book *An Unspoken Hunger*. "What was circling in my mind when I wrote the essays in *An Unspoken Hunger* was: How do we share this sense of the sacred, what Thoreau calls the 'active soul,' with our communities? How do we extend our notion of community to include all life-forms—plants, animals, rocks, rivers and human beings—and step forward with a compassionate intelligence?"

Williams lives with her husband, Brooke, above Salt Lake City in Emigration Canyon, along part of the original Mormon Trail followed by Brigham Young in 1847. She lives not far from her childhood home, which was on the edge of the city's foothills. It was her family who first nurtured her physical sense of nature and her part in it, says Williams. Her grandmother, Mimi, who also died of cancer, had an "enormous effect" on her understanding of nature.

I felt like I had my own spiritual teacher from the moment I was born. My grandmother would say, "Isn't this beautiful? Do you see this? How do you feel about this?" We would literally pour over the plates of birds at night and then I would dream about them. It was very physical, learning the birds on the page and then going out into nature and seeing them firsthand. Mimi would visit the ocean and bring the stories and the shells back to us. Again, very physical, learning about the ocean through natural storytelling and then actually holding the shells in the palms of our hands.

And her telescope. It was always set up in her front yard so we could see the planets, the moon. She was an extraordinary teacher. Mimi taught us about the interrelatedness of things. Once again, nothing in isolation.

When we were children, she would put on symphonies and have us paint on easels. We had art galleries. We thought we were stupendous. We would go to sleep at night knowing that in the morning around the table we would be asked what our dreams were. "You can remember if you try," Mimi would tell us.

So there was a great mythic sense about my grandmother. She was a student of Carl Jung, and in the midst of this traditional Mormon life, our grandmother would bring us the philosophies of the world.

And because we lived on the edge of the foothills, our games were always games of the imagination. We created a community called "Rock Town." We had a currency made of broken pieces of colored glass that we found in the mountains, and we had a secret language. My mother craved solitude, and after lunch we retreated to our bedrooms. From one to three o'clock we had quiet time. In the privacy of those hours we became very familiar with our own creativity.

Quiet is essential to me now. I can't imagine my life without it. It is also time not only alone but in the presence of Other, which for me is found in the natural world.

Being in nature is physical as well as spiritual. So much of what we experience in our lives takes place in the mind. Much of our society is staring at a computer screen, scanning the Internet, lost in cyberspace. Where will that lead us? If we lose our frame of reference to the natural world, to actual bedrock, we lose contact with who we are as animals. We can talk about the mind and the spirit, but we still largely perceive the world through our bodies, through flesh and bone and blood. That is what the land reminds us of, and I feel that is where that deep sense of humility comes from.

Brooke and I were at the Bird Refuge recently, to see the birds again, and the landscape and the levels of memories embedded there. We watched two avocets. I have never seen this in all the years I have been going to the Refuge—since I was a child. The female was standing in the water, with her wonderful thin blue legs, her white feathered body, black wings and rust head. She hunkered down and the male circled her in the marsh, baptizing her as he sprinkled her with water. He dipped his upturned bill in the lake and he sprinkled her around and around and around. He bowed, she bowed, and then they engaged in copulation.

To me this is an erotics of place. It is deeply physical. It is deeply spiritual. I don't think you can have one without the other. Even if it means we just have our hands in the soil. We may have to face the fact that we are an urban people, but we don't need to lose our contact with the land.

My greatest fear is that we really are losing our biological literacy. We no longer know the names of things. And if we lose the names of things, then they can disappear without thought or notice. What happens if we can no longer say "American avocet," "black-necked stilt," "bulrush," "cattail," "pickleweed"? What if we cannot name the ecosystems we belong to, if we cannot identify the communities in which we live and know whom we live among?

I was recently talking to Ted Strong, who is Yakima and the director of the Columbia River Intertribal Fisheries Commission. He told me that this year [1995] there were only 9,000 Chinook salmon in the Columbia River Basin where only 100 years ago the salmon were so abundant that people could walk across the river on the backs of the fish. Today, only 9,000 salmon. What does that mean?

What kind of inconsolable loneliness are we experiencing on a conscious and unconscious level? I think this is the grief that we intuitively feel. This is our unspoken hunger. How do we quell that? Perhaps this is the drug of consumerism and capitalism, our addiction to everything that tries to deaden and numb our senses to what we really feel, what we know in our hearts but fail to recognize or acknowledge.

Right now in Utah, we are engaged in very emotional discussions on wilderness. How much wilderness do we want? How much are we willing to have? There are those who say they want 5.7 million acres and are calling for "a tithe to creation." There are others who want no wilderness. They say environmentalism is one of the ugly spores that has broken off the giant fungus of communism, and that the United Nations Treaty on Biodiversity is the end of family values in America as we know them.

We hear others who say, "This land is our body. This land is what we love. This land is what we need for a healthy sustainable life." How do we reconcile these radically different philosophies?

I was listening to John Cobb, a theologian at Carlton College. He was talking about the various epics of human development through history. He looks at this century and sees World Wars I and II as classic examples of "Nationalism," which reached its devastating peak during the Holocaust and Hiroshima, and which then gave way to "Economism," which is where we are now. Then he sees us moving toward the next epic, which he calls "Earthism." He says that just as a holocaust caused us to move from nationalism to economism, to make the next leap, he fears we will need to experience some manner of deep suffering to move us from an economy-based philosophy such as capitalism to Earthism. He said, "What might that holocaust be?"

I thought, "We are in the middle of it, with the wholesale degradation of the planet, whether it is the loss of the rain forest or overgrazing in the American West."

The loss of biodiversity is a holocaust on a scale we cannot imagine or comprehend. It is merely an abstraction. But it won't be for long. Our great hubris as a species is that we are separate, immune from other forms of life. We no longer believe in the connectedness of things.

But we do know the linkages of nature in our own bodies. I was in Iowa talking to women who are farmers. One woman's father was dead from leukemia and her children had many health problems. She said, "Look at my rabbits. They are full of tumors. DuPont says there is no problem with our water." And she cupped the water in her hands and said, "This water is poisonous. I don't need the facts. I know what I see within my own family. I know what I feel in my own body."

I think about Breyten Breytenbach, the South African poet who has worked for years against apartheid and spent several years in prison. We were in Mexico City at a symposium about environmental degradation and social change. I asked him, "If we are interested in a revolution of the spirit, an evolution of the spirit, what do we do?" And he looked at me dead on and said directly, "You Americans, you have mastered the art of living with the unacceptable." And he walked away.

His words have become a mantra for me. I think that is why women in particular have the capacity to organize around issues of social justice. This is the truth of our lives. This is what we know. This is what we stand for. And this is what we stand against.

I think that is what I was trying to say in the essay, "The Wild Card," in Unspoken Hunger. *Perhaps the most radical act we can commit is to stay home. Commit to a place. Someone must be there to chart the changes, so when the Chinook salmon no longer come up the river, we can say, "There are no more salmon." It's like the farm women who are standing their ground in Iowa in the places they love. They are organizing around issues of health and the environment. It is the women who are saying, "We will not be marginalized. Our social, health and environmental issues are issues of dignity, and for too long they have been relegated to the periphery, ghettoized. No longer.*

These are issues of sustainability, and as women, as mothers, as wives, we know this intuitively. We know this instinctively."

Again, we have to ask the question, "What are we afraid of?" Women speak with snakes. The metaphor of the snake shows us over and over again that we have the capacity to be split open, pulled apart, to shed old skins and then grow another.

We can be both compassionate and fierce at once. A full range. It is a sacred rage born out of love and loss that we possess. Our challenge today—as perhaps it has always been—is how do we live and love with a broken heart? How do we engage in community and still find time to replenish what we give away?

And the earth shows us how again and again.

We constantly need to ask, "What can I let go of and what can I bring into my life?" I think these kinds of questions and assessments can only be made in solitude.

Quiet and solitude are essential to me. I can't imagine my life without them. And I need both extremes of solitude. I can need as little as a hot bath for 10 minutes or the solace of a prayer. Or I can need an absolute pilgrimage—days, weeks, even months where I am not available. Like a fox, I have learned how to disappear.

I pattern my life like the cycles of nature. I like that because it makes me feel tied to the seasons. And I really do take my cue from animals. In the fall there is a deepening of the soul, and I do go underground like a bear and don't engage in public life. It is time to be home, time with Brooke, a time of reflection and reading and writing. Of course, there are exceptions. Life cannot be so rigid. There are always obligations to family. But my intention is to slow down, stay put—and I do hold to it as much as I can.

In the spring, I emerge. I hear the birds outside our windows. I open them, and watch the aspens leaf. I realize I am ready to come out into the world, that something has been gleaned from those winter months, from that time of hibernation, from that dreamtime of the bear. Spring is the season I give to my community. It is a public time of planting and gathering. And summer is total joy. That is the time Brooke and I give to each other—being out in the garden, on the land—when we remember the generosity of life around us. I commit to one writing workshop so I have time with students. That is how I try to choreograph the year.

I think we are all hungry to live a life of greater intention, a life of greater meaning, greater simplicity—a life that is rich internally, not just materially. But my concern, what I am completely obsessed with, is that we talk about a spiritual life and yet we systematically destroy our very source of holiness, which is the Earth, the land, the animals. That is why I think spiritual concerns must be rooted in pragmatic solutions. And that is why I am an activist, why I will forever be standing my ground in the places I love. Wilderness is not a luxury. It is an absolute necessity, one on which our mental, physical and spiritual health depends.

I was so moved to be in Hiroshima recently. This was the 50th anniversary of when we dropped the atomic bomb. I met a woman there, Dr. Shoko Itoh. Interestingly, I think two of the books that meant the most to me growing up were John Hershey's Hiroshima and Thoreau's Walden. Shortly after I'd read both of them, my mother was diagnosed with breast cancer, in 1971. Almost 25 years later, I found myself in Hiroshima with Dr. Itoh, who is a Thoreauvian scholar. There we were with mothers who'd both had cancer, both of us with the legacy of the atomic bomb in our bones, both of us Hibakusha—which translates to "explosion-affected people."

She took me to an island called Miyajima. As we took the boat across, she said, "Everything on this island is Divine. It is usually covered with mist, appearing vague like the Japanese."

We walked through the forest on the island until we came to a shrine. A wonderful, huge orange gate stands as an entrance to the ocean. We stood on the edge of the shrine with our backs to the sea, looking out to the forest and she said, "We say that healing comes through the hands of man. May I take your hand? We say my energy will flow through your hand and heal you and your energy will flow through your hand into mine and heal me and together we can move forward and heal the world."

"I couldn't begin to say what other women should be doing when they start to question their lives. I can only say what I do when I am in that situation. I stop, I slow down and I listen. I think the pace of our lives is so frenetic that it doesn't allow us to assess that which is essential. We lose our souls in the process. I know for me, when I feel my life is out of balance, I have to stop and go out to the lake or the desert of southern Utah. In the short term, I go into the bathtub, light a candle and shut the door. And I close my eyes.

"But often the answer isn't to stop everything and shut the door. Instead we need to ask, 'What is feeding me?' Perhaps stopping what we are doing isn't as important as adding the things that feed us so a balance is restored. It may mean gathering a bouquet of flowers from the garden, or sitting down and reading a poem, or having tea with a beloved friend or taking a walk. For me, solitude is my source of rejuvenation, nature is my source of renewal. Without them, I would go mad."

ALEXANDRA STODDARD

Author, lecturer, interior designer
and television host of
Homes Across America

*"Once you realize you're not afraid of death, that
death is inevitable, you see that focusing on death
isn't important while we are here. What's important is
focusing on living and breathing, and keeping the fire
in our belly, and keeping our energy high so we can
make the world a more vital place for others."*

F or millions of us, Alexandra Stoddard is akin to a wise and intimate friend who guides us to discover gracious, compassionate and purposeful lives in these fragmented times. When our lifestyles smother our very souls and drive us perilously close to our spiritual breaking points, Stoddard helps us be better stewards of our time, energies, resources—and spirits.

A talented interior designer and author of 15 bestselling books, including *Creating a Beautiful Home, Living Beautifully Together* and *The Art of the Possible*, Stoddard stresses that the soul needs beauty to flourish. She shows how weaving art, music, grace and rituals into our daily lives can refresh us for our life's work.

Making Choices: The Joy of a Courageous Life, one of Stoddard's most personal books, is a worthy compass to living a fulfilling, affirmative life. It chronicles her inner searching when, at 50, she began to review the difficult choices that defined her life. Sharing private moments, from her divorce to her struggles with siblings, Stoddard intimately explores the philosophies that guide and sustain her life in the midst of personal tragedy. She has learned a great deal, she says, about the risks and responsibilities that come with freedom of choice.

"I do feel that I am on a mission, which is to help people to understand that they can just let go, be themselves and then do their best. Life is difficult, you can be tired, and that's okay. You can cancel appointments, and that's okay. And you can mess up, and that's okay. You can say no to one more demand that's just too much and not feel guilty about it. I think the guilt robs you of any potential for joy in life."

Stoddard's words resonate with a well-honed wisdom earned by making difficult choices. Twenty years ago, for instance, Stoddard was divorced and caught up in raising two young daughters and building her career. She also was pressured by her mother to take more responsibility for her mentally ill brother. Given her overwhelming commitments and concerns, Stoddard bowed to her internal wisdom and determined that she could—but should not—bear the responsibility for her brother's pain or choices. When he committed suicide years later, in her grief, she again concluded she had made the right choice, recognizing that her brother had been an independent human being, with motivations, thoughts and pain she never knew and never could know.

Other personal sadness, such as the loss of close friends, has shown her that our sorrows etch great openings for joy. "I've had an amazing life, an incredible life. I think I've had a wonderful mix of great sorrow and great pain, and I'm not as afraid of pain as a lot of people are. I think many people haven't had enough pain in their lives to know what joy is."

That sense of joy grew in her mother's flower garden when, as a child, Stoddard felt herself open up to the wondrous spiritual magic of flowers. "When I was three years old, I had this 'Moment of Being' that Virginia Woolf talked about in a book by that name. This awakening was so strong, it lifted me up to a state of elevated awareness where, though I couldn't read or write, flowers became my language and communicated to me through color. So wherever I go in the world, I always feel the sorrow, suffering and pain of the people from the colors and textures of the surroundings where people live. And it started in my mother's flower garden when I discovered this power in nature, color and beauty. I am very Emersonian in my faith that way."

At 16, Stoddard's spirituality was nurtured when her aunt,

Elizabeth Johns, a pioneering international social worker, took her around the world, exposing her to architecture, design and beauty—as well as sorrow and suffering—in such places as Europe, India, Pakistan, Sri Lanka, Burma, the Philippines, Hong Kong and Japan. The eye-opening journey to 32 cities in 13 different countries molded Stoddard's view of life, the connectedness of all things—and her own future. "I knew then that I had a calling. I knew I was a leader. I understand people's sorrow and pain. I've suffered too and I know that we're all in this together. And if we are brave and courageous, we can feel joy in our lives. Together we can help each other on this earthly journey."

Stoddard says her existence now is grounded by living in a constant state of awareness of her higher self. Her favorite maxim is Lao Tzu's "The way to do is to be." To find the joy in simply being, she advises women to indulge their souls in regular times of solitude and meditation, moments for balance and inward gazing. "If we're angry, that is temporary insanity. That is not our higher self. If we're jealous or envious, we're off our path."

Stoddard lives in New York City and Stonington Village, Connecticut, with her husband, Peter Megargee Brown, a trial lawyer, lecturer and author. She has two grown daughters.

Because we haven't mentored, nurtured and cared for each other well enough, Stoddard says our spiritual natures hunger for greater nourishment.

We have a burning hunger, a burning hunger. It's not a religious zealot feeling. It's not a feeling that, "There's one way, or one path." But I think people have become so confused because they've lost the light on their paths.

If people would go to a place and gather together, sing or dance, hold hands or talk together, the community, the feeling and the energy from that would vibrate through their souls and heal them. They wouldn't get such a kick out of a violent gun.

Whenever harm is done to one of us, it's done to us all. I think of life as a mirror. If I hurt you, I've wounded myself far more than I've hurt you. Spirituality is our only potential for healing.

I think we all have a spiritual urge, a compulsion to risk and lead a spiritual life. Our higher self is always there just smiling at us, waiting for us to wake up. We don't have to go anywhere, do anything or spend money.

We just have to realize we're all spiritual and any denial of that is denial. We're here for a very short period of time on this planet earth, so universally we have to face the reality that we can seek immortality in our good deeds, our children, in the books we write and in the lives that we affect in a positive way.

And I think there is such a thing as universal truth and a reason for each one of us to be here. We just have to figure it out!

I ended Choices with a quote from Julian of Norwich, who lived in the 15th century and who is often regarded as the "first English woman of letters." She said, "But all shall be well and all shall be well, and all manner of thing shall be well." We must remember we were each born with a Divine spark, and that's our gift. A spark of divinity. It's already been given us. It's already inside us.

But everyone has to discover this his or her own way. We each have to question, doubt and struggle. People have gone to monasteries for thousands of years and said, "Master, master, I am not enlightened." And the master will say, "Well, have you heard the birds sing? Have you seen the apple blossoms?"

In other words, you have to understand that your journey is not my journey. There is not one prayer book, one meditation book or one Bible. We all have to continue to grow, struggle and stretch our intellectual and spiritual muscles until the very, very last day. Everyone has to figure out what it is that makes them strive toward their highest being. And the only way we can do that is through action.

It's always action-oriented. Have you noticed that? Aristotle spoke of active virtue. Our actions represent our spirit. Watch a child skip or an adult sing. We act out of a need to connect, to share our humanity. I learn about myself through my thousands of acts. What's most fascinating is that more and more, I'm in an elevated awareness where I don't even consciously think of my-self, my separateness. When I'm alone, when I am with family and loved ones, I not only try to stay on my path, but I attempt to be the best I can be, to stretch to my greatest potential and to remain grateful for the great gift of the miracle of my life.

How you spend your time, what you read, what you do when you're alone, whom you love and how you earn a living all act upon your spirit. The more good actions, the healthier and hap-pier the journey. I think joy is something that happens when you are able to not be narcissistic, to forget about yourself and your age and to go about your journey—which is always, when you are trying to live up to your higher self, one that is helping others.

But I will go down to the end not telling anyone else how to find their spiritual journey. I will guide them to books they should read. I will tell them to light candles and have flowers in front of them. And I will tell them to be in solitude to meditate, to receive their higher message regularly. And to calm down.

And what I know about my own life—I don't know how other people feel—I know I just feel better when I wake in the morning, meditate, have quiet time, think about what is true and beautiful and lovely, read spiritual books, listen to beautiful music, light candles and do everything with a sense of pure grace. Even the baths I take, the soaps I use, the flowers I surround myself with lend themselves to an aesthetic and spiritual life.

Flowers are my metaphor for God reminding us that our lives are fragile and precious. We have to be there to smell the rose and observe it before it wilts and withers, because we're going to wilt and wither, too. It's sort of Zen mixed in with everything else: "Be here now."

So try not to be without something growing. Even if you're in a cement jungle, have a bulb you can plant or grow. Nurture a plant or something that's alive to remind you of how fragile life is. You have to be a gardener in life to know about spirituality.

I believe that we share energy. There's energy coming into us through a Divine presence of God in our daily lives, and people just have to wake up. You don't have to wear religious garb. You don't have to light candles in cathedrals at 5 o'clock in the *morning. You don't have to sing hymns and say psalms—though it might be good for you.*

The ultimate thing we must tap into is the fact that when we no longer have our physical life, have we lived? Have we appreciated? Have we been grateful? Have we used our gifts and talents to our highest potential so that we can then, in turn, be part of the Divine creation?

"I urge everyone to 'time tithe,' which is to take 10 percent of their daily lives—which is really only about nine hours a week for the waking hours—and use that time for contemplation. This morning I woke up at 2 A.M. because we were having a blizzard and it was really beautiful. I spent two hours looking out the window, and that was my prayer."

NIKKI GIOVANNI

Poet, English professor and author

"A spiritual life is never what's happened to us. That's the easiest thing in the world to deal with. It's dealing with what we have done to others that's difficult."

Perhaps one of the most widely read poets of our time, Nikki Giovanni has for 30 years traced that precarious line of exposing humanity's wounds while illuminating its finest achievements. From its militant roots in the 1960s to its maturity today, Giovanni's writing has always targeted hypocrisy, mean-spiritedness and injustice, while lauding the power of nobility, kindness and integrity.

When she was a young girl, Giovanni's parents and grand-parents instilled in her the sense that individual action and moral imperative can shape the world. Her grandmother especially fired her strong sense of responsibility for her actions and her commitment to her community.

"I was trained intellectually and spiritually to respect myself and the people who respect me. I was emotionally trained to love those who love me," Giovanni wrote in her autobiography, *Gemini.* Her collection of 20 books also includes *Racism 101, Black Feeling, Black Talk, Black Judgement, My House, Cotton Candy on a Rainy Day, Sacred Cows…and Other Edibles* and *The Women and the Men.*

Woven through her writing is the desire to nurture connec-tions, tolerate our inevitable quirks and differences, speak the truth, no matter how painful, and dream big. We are all capable of tremendous beauty, of giving love and of making the world what we want it to be, says Giovanni, who first wanted to be a social worker.

"I just think everybody has something to give. Everybody has something they can put back into people, whether it's being patient with older people or choosing to help someone else out. I have volunteered all my life, at schools, in retirement homes—I serve on a couple of boards—all of which I find very enjoyable."

Giovanni is now a professor of English at Virginia Polytechnic Institute and State University. The mother of a grown son, Thomas, she hopes her work has helped draw humanity closer. As she wrote in one essay, "I love it when people say they have read my poetry. . . . I just thank them because whether I disappointed or delighted them, they took the time to be involved in my effort . . . to explore with me . . . to extend themselves to me as I have extended myself to them.

"It's lonely. Writing. But so is practicing tennis or football runs. So is studying. So is waxing the floor and changing the baby. So is life. We are less lonely when we connect. Art is a connection. I like being a link. I hope the chain will hold."

Giovanni defines a spiritual life as one lived with dignity, integrity and respect for others.

I do think that's a broad-based definition of spirituality. What I like to use is the term "civilization." Obviously, we as human beings are a little short of civilizing one another, but it's clearly one thing we are working on. We are trying to improve our ability to function within units and then again within larger units.

That's the history of the world. But when we get in larger units, civilized behavior breaks down. People who are terribly sensitive about being women are horribly racist. We are slow, we are not a bright species. Certainly our emotional growth for 300 years has lagged considerably behind our intellectual and spiritual pursuits.

The whole idea of living in a hierarchical mode, of having a top dog or top bitch, that has to stop. Do we really think that is a good idea? Friends should be friends. We should respect people with whom we work.

To me, being spiritual is so very basic. We've lost basic politeness—for instance, saying "Please" if you want something. Saying "Thank you" if you get it. If you are nice to someone, you are considered a patsy fool.

People are important to me. I am 51 years old, and I think it's fair to say I've not been abusive with anybody. I hate people who holler at the waiter in a restaurant. I dislike it not just because it's bad manners, but because it's totally unnecessary. You are just living for a while, and then you are gone. This life is finite. I think human beings are the most fascinating creatures. We can get so convoluted about the most ordinary things, like traffic delays at the airport. What's the big deal? You are only going to be here for a few years.

And I do know we put too much emphasis on money. I have nothing against people earning their weight. We must have a method of exchange for goods and labor. But there are too many people thinking, "I don't have enough."

If I could do anything on earth, it would be to get people to recognize that the earth is alive. Whatever we are doing to the earth, we are doing to a living thing. Hopefully this will stop some people from being indifferent to each other and to living beings. Hopefully it will get people to stop dumping poisons in water. We should take only as much as we need. The earth is a living thing and has to be treated with that respect. I have no problem with the idea that we are connected to the earth.

I think people are supposed to be happy. We are here for such a finite period of time. I know in your adult years you become more aware of how finite it is, so you ought to be doing something enjoyable. I think all of us have something we can do to bring us joy. Ninety percent of what drives people nuts is that they don't find their own "quilt" to make. They spend all of their time doing something they don't like.

A lot of people try to convince themselves that what they like to do is insufficient. If you like to quilt, and all your friends say, "But you have a master's degree," you should change your friends. I don't think it's so hard to know what you like to do. It's just hard to go against the flow. If I am spiritual, it's because I do what I like.

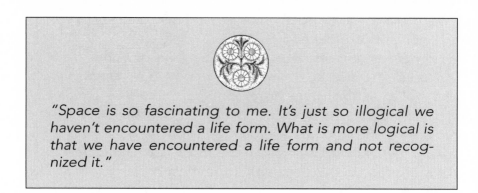

"Space is so fascinating to me. It's just so illogical we haven't encountered a life form. What is more logical is that we have encountered a life form and not recognized it."

CORINNE McLAUGHLIN

Author and cofounder of Sirius, a spiritual community and ecological village in Massachusetts

"We need to find the grain of truth on both sides of an issue, raising our problems to a higher level of synthesis."

I n the 1960s, Corinne McLaughlin was a lightning rod for political activism. While she attended the University of California, Berkeley and UCLA, she fought for racial equality, women's rights, environmental reform and other issues. But when she stepped back and looked at social progress, she realized the results of her and her colleagues' efforts often fell short of their dreams. Slowly, McLaughlin began to question her work and realized it might be more effective to direct the lightning inward, transforming herself first.

"I had been involved with changing the world politically since I was 12 years old and first watched the political conventions. But my spiritual exploration came after a period of intense political activism. I felt we weren't as effective as we wanted to be because we weren't dealing with the deeper causes of issues and affecting change on a profound, personal level."

Raised in a traditional Catholic family, McLaughlin began to study Eastern and Western traditions, metaphysical teachings and ancient philosophies that embraced the interconnectedness of life. She concluded that since we are all inherently part of one another, we must first strengthen our internal spiritual selves before we can bring about the massive changes needed by our society. "We must transform ourselves if we intend to transform the world."

In the 1970s, McLaughlin spent three years at the Scottish spiritual-ecological community, Findhorn. It was there that she taught herself to meditate. "That experience was the single most transforming factor of my life. I have been meditating for the last 20 years, for about 30 minutes each day, to create the quiet time to contact my inner source of guidance and to find that wisdom inside each of us. The Divine Presence inside me, the Inner Teacher, or whatever name you call it, has been very key for me. It has helped me be more peaceful. It has helped me get a clear sense of my direction in life, my purpose, my service to the world."

That sense of service now drives McLaughlin to bring more compassion, goodness, ethical responsibility and humanity to the world. In 1978, she and Gordon Davidson founded Sirius, a spiritual community and ecological village in Massachusetts. Sirius is also a respected center and model community for sustainable research and development, with educational programs on organic gardening, energy-efficient technologies, solar building and affordable housing.

McLaughlin and Davidson are active in Washington, D.C., and in regional Northeast politics, helping diverse organizations and interests find solutions to social problems. They recently published *Spiritual Politics*, a clarion call for a new synthesis of politics and spirituality, to allow opposing views to reach consensus based on the highest good.

The book applies many metaphysical teachings to world affairs, illustrating that negative, hateful thoughts and emotions, for instance, affect not only personal health but the collective health of a society. Even one spiritually motivated individual with the intention to do good can dramatically effect political change, McLaughlin says. "Understanding this is tremendously empowering, for it helps us to realize that we no longer have to be victims of powerful political forces we don't fully understand or control. What we do and what we think affects every other living being in the web of life."

The key, McLaughlin believes, is for each of us to recognize our power to bring more harmony and compassion to the world, using our inner resources to effect outer change. What is regarded as mystical and metaphysical today will become tomorrow's common-sense wisdom, she maintains.

I think we have greater inner power to affect the world than we realize. What I have seen is that instead of sitting there and feeling powerless about what's going on in the world politically, we can instead go inward to a place of stillness. We can align with our soul, the inner divinity, the wise being within us, and ask for help in a particular crisis situation. We can visualize white light and love pouring into the situation. We can send love to those individuals who are victims of war, floods, fires or conflicts.

I visualize people resolving conflicts and finding common ground. Instead of criticizing our political leaders, I visualize them aligning with their highest self and with higher spiritual principles. We do need to see clearly what our problems are and not ignore the problems with our leaders. We can still let them know when they are doing something wrong.

But in our minds we can also hold them in our prayers, send them love and light and see them acting out of their highest motives. We can send positive energy, light and love to our president, to Congress, the Supreme Court and all branches of government. One thing we recommend is the "adopt a leader program." Pick someone who has a lot of potential but needs help, and hold him or her in your prayers and meditations.

We need to take spiritual approaches to political problems. One example of a spiritual approach is President Clinton's Council on Sustainable Development, which is a new way to build a consensus among adversaries. The council includes members of the Cabinet and chief executive officers of major corporations and environmental and social justice groups. In one year, they formed a consensus on 15 principles for sustainable development.

This consensus-building is happening everywhere, even in the abortion question, where adversaries who were once polarized are finding common ground. I have seen this work in local areas, such as in Oregon, where loggers and environmentalists are trying to find common ground. This approach is very spiritual. This is what we need to do more. As we grow in wisdom, we learn there are often good people and a grain of truth on both sides of an issue.

You can't solve a problem on the same level that created the problem. You have to take it to a higher level of consciousness. To me that is what a spiritual approach to problem-solving is all about.

I think we constantly have to try to stay detached from problems and ask ourselves what we are learning from crisis. The Native Americans talk about "reading the Book of Life." In the environment, we are certainly learning that we are taking the natural world for granted.

We are seeing our interconnection when pollution drifts downstream and goes across borders, affecting all of us. The environment shows us that interconnectedness is real and not just a vague metaphysical idea. At Findhorn, we learned we can help heal the environment by co-creatively working with the inner forces of nature. Whether you call these forces Devas, Angels or Kachinas, as the Native Americans do, we can work with them to help the deserts bloom, to create new species of plants and to get insects to leave plants without killing them. We have seen this happen on a small scale at Findhorn and Sirius. There is no environmental situation we can't change if we understand the inner science of it.

We have to work with the forces of light, knowing that the purpose of the forces of darkness is to test and strengthen us. Down through the ages there have always been forces of light and forces of darkness. I feel the real evil is found in those who work to divide and conquer us, who keep us separate from each other. It is found in those who keep us focused on materialism, so that our only concern is how much money we have and how many possessions we have. It is found in forces that work to create fear and anger and stir up negative emotions, appealing to people's basest instincts. The forces of darkness also work to enslave humanity. They don't respect free will. Those who manipulate your free will aren't of the light because free will is sacred.

This is done on an inner energy level. Just as there are saints and masters in our world who work with light, there are beings who are intentionally choosing to work with darkness and who will sell their souls for power. This is real, it happens, and we see this reported in the media every day. But it is never too late to turn back to the light. It is up to us to distinguish good from evil and know in the end that good ultimately triumphs.

As humanity is evolving, things are getting better. More nations are at peace than ever before. Violence and illness in many countries are down. We are growing in wisdom and good people are coming together from both sides of conflicts to learn to work together. The majority of our political leaders are well-intentioned, but we need to help them align with their highest self so they can serve the good of the whole rather than just their own personal interests.

"Meditation is a key to spiritual growth in whatever tradition you learn it. Even if you just sit silently for 15 minutes a day and learn to listen to God, it is beneficial. Clear out your thoughts, breathe in, feel the peace within. Practice stepping back and being a detached observer of your thoughts and feelings.

"When you feel yourself getting angry, if you just step back and observe it, it helps release the anger. If you practice this in meditation, then you can do it more easily during the day. Actively explore. Read inspirational books. Go to spiritual lectures. But don't feel you have to pay a lot of money or totally surrender your will to a teacher, group or cult to be spiritual. That is not the way it works. I would question anything that promises you instant enlightenment in a weekend."

BETTY EADIE

Author and expert on
near-death experiences

"To live a spiritual life is to come as close as possible to knowing our higher self and the God-like qualities inherent in each of us. A spiritual life has a strange pull, almost like gravity, pulling us closer to our creator."

The daughter of a Sioux Indian mother, Betty Eadie was raised in rural Nebraska and on the Rosebud Indian Reservation in South Dakota. She was the seventh of 10 children. When she was four, her parents separated and her mother went back to live on the reservation. Her father, a fair-haired Scots-Irishman, left to live with his parents. Eadie and six of her siblings were placed in a Catholic boarding school.

The first winter at the school, she became gravely ill with whooping cough and pneumonia. Burning with a fever, she remembers slipping in and out of sleep. When she awoke, she heard a doctor saying, "It's too late. We've lost her." As the doctor walked away, she sensed yet another presence and felt a new sensation. A man with a beautiful white beard was rocking her gently, soothing her with his soft touch and calming her with the love that flowed from his beaming face. Eadie had no idea who he was, but she remembers never wanting to leave him.

When she regained consciousness, the man with the white beard was gone—yet the experience ignited her search for greater spirituality. She continued to question the meaning of life and the nature of God throughout her adult life. Then, at 31, she underwent a hysterectomy, after which she experienced her second near-death experience.

Eadie's experience with death allowed her to feel God's love as extremely approachable, enveloping and never-ending. "In return," she says, "all we can do is create as much love as we can within ourselves and our surroundings. That love must include all things and all people, charity for others, kindness and generosity. Above all else, as it was told to me, we must love one another. And when we do that, everything else will fall into place."

The mother of eight children and grandmother of eight, Eadie now enjoys worldwide acclaim since the publication of her account of her near-death experience in the bestselling book, *Embraced by the Light*. The book was on the *New York Times* hardcover bestseller list for 78 weeks, and was also on the *New York Times* paperback bestseller list for many weeks. *Embraced by the Light* has now sold more than 5.5 million copies.

Eadie states that her experience of God has given her great tranquility and peace in her life. It has also given her profound insights into her own spirituality, which continues to evolve.

When we go deep within ourselves, we cannot help but feel at peace. All the right answers are there. To come closer to God is to achieve a balance between the flesh and spirit. If we don't find that peace, it causes unrest and sorrow in our lives. That is what is happening in so much of the world today. Not enough people are at peace with themselves.

God is foremost in my life. To project that concept, I must maintain a large measure of peace within myself. I know that God is love, and if I do not have and recognize that same love within me, it will be most difficult to express that love to others.

So I seek out the spirit of God daily. At various times over the years, I've used touchstones to help me do this, but touchstones often aren't available to us. And there will come a time when they will not be available at all. The only touchstone we will have will be our internal connection with God. Physical things are easily lost and can change with the waves of life. I know some people have come to accept various touchstones as their physical connection to God, but to me, that's not much different than building "golden images." However, if that is what you need at a point in time to connect with God, that's okay!

I have found a place within my heart where I go to be with God daily. That place is available to me any time I choose. Though time is precious, you need to take the first few minutes of the morning and the last few minutes at night for prayer. It can be as elaborate a prayer or as simple a prayer as you choose. If you will take the time and develop that prayerful habit, this will bring you closer to God and bring about a new behavior pattern.

Also, we are all at our best when we are most giving to others. When we are self-centered, love is difficult to find. Love is like electricity, a current, an energy, and when you turn it on and allow it to flow through you, it must flow out to others that you touch. It's like a giving and a receiving—when you give to someone, the love literally flows through you, and then you cannot help but feel that love.

When I get up each day, I put my life in God's hands and say aloud, "Today I prefer to serve God in every way I can." We don't know what our life's mission is. We must remain open. Your spirit knows that you are on the right path when you make a decision you feel good about. You receive an energy that propels you along that particular path. When you act in a way contrary to that path, you stumble and feel uncertain. Then it is time to sit down and reflect.

People talk about finding their life's purpose. I don't know that we are all to know our purposes. You might sense that you know another's life purpose. When they seem to be right on, you can look at them and say, "Oh, they are certainly doing what they were created to do. They are doing what God wants them to do." And you might yearn for that moment when you find your particular niche in life.

I don't believe that you really know what your own life purpose is. People often say my book is my purpose, but I have never felt that the book was my total reason for being here on earth. I keep looking every day for that reason. However, I think rather than trying to find out what it might be, I prefer to keep myself positioned or prepared for whatever comes. I guess I don't want to miss out on anything.

I believe God's plan is so much grander than anything we could envision for ourselves. It encompasses all. So there is a particular reason to be where we are right now. One reason might be for our personal growth and spiritual development. But we are also here collectively as well. We are all a piece of the entire puzzle of life.

Since what we do affects everyone, rather than delving into "Why am I here?" perhaps we should just be the best we can be and leave ourselves open to be accessed by God. God is perfect in everything—so everyone here was perfectly Divine from the beginning! It is when we have removed ourselves from Him that we lose balance and focus and become imperfect. We are here to learn to love, and our connection with God will help us do that if we let Him.

The more knowledge I receive, and the more I understand about my own spirituality and the spirituality of others, the more I struggle to obtain yet more knowledge. There is just more to know. It's very complex. It's almost as though ignorance is truly bliss. Once you become aware of something, it opens a door. You walk though that door, then there are more doors you have to choose from. You select yet another door, walk through that one, and there are even more doors to choose from. It's a constant challenge and a constant process.

So whenever we reach a point where we think we are fully developed spiritually, we must be careful lest we find we are really caught in a maze and that we have dead-ended. We must never cease to seek more truth, knowledge and the understanding of God and His love.

"God is approachable. He likes that one-on-one in our communications with Him. God wants us to have both spiritual and material things. Nothing is wrong with asking. And you can be specific. God wants that. It is good to define what your needs are. How else will you know what you want? God knows your prayer before you pray it, anyway! Above all else, love one another. This is my message."

NELL NEWMAN

Head of Newman's Own Organics

"Growing up in the Connecticut countryside surrounded by nature, I learned through observation about the balance of my own little ecosystem. What I saw over those years gave me a deep respect and understanding for nature's intrinsic equilibrium as well as mankind's effect on it."

T he average child receives four times more exposure than adults to widely used cancer-causing pesticides in food. Pesticides may cause an extra 1.4 million cancer cases among Americans. It's estimated that anywhere from 27,000 to 300,000 farm workers are poisoned annually by pesticides.

These are just some of the grim statistics surrounding agri-culture's reliance on chemicals, part of the "chemical barrage hurled against the fabric of life" that environmentalist Rachel Carson warned of. But often, knowing the truth intellectually isn't enough to make us change. Sometimes we are most moved to act from our own experiences, even that of biting into a tasty salty pretzel, says Nell Newman.

Head of Newman's Own Organics, Newman has created an organic pretzel so that consumers literally taste the merits of chemical-free farming. The three-year-old venture is her way of giving back.

"The idea of the organic food division didn't come to me in a 'flash of bright light.' Rather, it was born out of my frustration with agribusiness and the conventional agricultural system, and their detrimental effects on our environment and health."

In 1995, with Newman's Own Organics in its second year of sales, it gives her great pleasure to show those who said it couldn't be done, Newman says. "Our success allows me the opportunity to set an example by returning something to society and the environment, an example I learned from my parents when they began Newman's Own 12 years ago.

"As Papa explains it, he looked at his good fortune in life as 'the luck of the draw.' So when he began Newman's Own, he felt obliged to return something to society rather than put the profits in his pocket. When I began Newman's Own Organics, it just seemed like the right thing to do, and it gave me the opportunity to follow in my father's footsteps."

She joined those footsteps after loading a suitcase full of organic produce and flying from California to Connecticut to make her family's Thanksgiving dinner. After her family ate the organic potatoes, salad, range-fed turkey and pumpkin pie, Nell leaned over and asked her dad, "How did you like your organic Thanksgiving dinner?"

Now Nell and "Pa," with overalls and pitchfork, beam in American Gothic style from the bags of Newman's Own Organic pretzels. Following the example of Newman's Own, which has already given $62 million to charities, all after-tax profits for Newman's Own Organics also go to charitable causes.

For two years, Newman has been traveling the country, from trade shows to conferences, touting the benefits of sustainable, chemical-free agriculture. Her scientific background—she has a degree in human ecology from the College of the Atlantic in Bar Harbor, Maine—immediately elevates her credibility with the agriculture and food industries. That training, combined with her early upbringing in then rural Connecticut, gives Newman a deep understanding of the effects of chemicals on our interconnected ecosystem.

"When I was growing up, I spent as much time as possible in the woods turning over rocks, inspecting what lived under them and fishing in the river that ran through our backyard. Over the years, I watched as 'my' river slowly declined in direct correlation with the increase in houses built along its banks. Most of these homes, including our own, drew water from the river to water their lawns, eventually decreasing the flow. Added on top were the chemicals from traditional gardening practices, and the river succumbed to an increase in nitrogen and various pesticides."

Newman estimates the river's biodiversity has been more than halved in the 30 years that her family has lived there. "Although it still appears to be a quaint New England stream, it is nowhere as diverse or prolific as when I was a kid. That was my earliest experience with the interconnectedness of nature and the effect people have when they neglect their environment. For me, nature provides an opportunity to learn about the ebb and flow that ecosystems go through as they seek equilibrium. We have much to learn from the earth if we take the time to listen and observe carefully."

After college, Newman worked at the Environmental Defense Fund in New York and with the Ventana Wilderness Sanctuary, which helped reestablish the bald eagle in central California. Newman also was a fund raiser for the Santa Cruz Predatory Bird Research Group. First learning about chemicals' impact on birds of prey steeled her for a lifetime as an environmental activist.

As a child, I was always mesmerized by birds, in particular birds of prey. One of my favorites was the peregrine falcon, known for its ability to dive at speeds of up to 200 miles an hour. When I began to read I realized that this amazing falcon, which I admired so, had become almost extinct in the United States due to the use of DDT.

Although I guess I was aware that mankind has been responsible for the extinction of many species before my time, the thought that it was happening in the present, during my lifetime, was mind-boggling for a child of 10. That was one of the reasons I later become involved with the peregrine falcon restoration programs carried out by the Peregrine Fund and the Santa Cruz Predatory Bird Research Group (SCPBRG). Over the years, I've conducted two release sites, one in Idaho and one in Vermont, and later became a board member of the Peregrine Fund.

Now after releasing more than 800 peregrine falcons in California over a 15-year period, the SCPBRG at the University of California has established more than 120 breeding pairs. Although the population has been increasing the past two years, the question of the long-term sustainability of this population still exists. Across the rest of the nation, the peregrine falcon population has done well, but because California is an agricultural state, we are now finding new contaminants in the peregrine eggs, from PCBs and dioxins to the still-present DDT. It took decades for biologists to discover exactly how DDT was affecting the peregrines' reproductive ability. What will be the effect of these new contaminants?

To me, the most disconcerting problem is the difficulty in raising funds from federal or private sources to monitor this population to insure its sustainability and to make sure we are there if it fails. The reestablishment of the peregrine falcon was one of the first endangered species success stories, and it is extremely shortsighted to presume its success in this state under the present environmental conditions.

Over the years, examples such as this made me more and more interested in organic agriculture as an alternative to conventional farming practices. I realize organic farming will not always be feasible in every type of farming situation. But how will we know unless we give it a try? We still have the same amount of pests we had 40 years ago. We just use twice as much pesticides to kill them. The federal government spends $1 billion per year on conventional agricultural research. Just imagine how far along we'd be if the government spent as much on organic farming techniques.

After so many years avoiding the public eye, I'm now much more comfortable in my role as an educator and spokesperson for organic farming. To me, it's an important issue to understand because of the long-term benefits for the planet. It's extremely gratifying because my work has a ripple effect.

We support the growth of organic farming through the use of our ingredients, which in turn promote a cleaner environment, less erosion and a more pristine workplace for farmers *and their workers. Then we get to donate our profits to charity. It's a multifaceted approach that embodies the interconnectedness of life. Sometimes I'm amazed people don't see the big picture and how they themselves fit into this environment. But then perhaps my perspective is different because I was raised in the country and got a biology degree. I had the pleasure of growing up in the woods, wading through streams, fishing and watching the wonders of nature unfold. I don't think there was ever a time I wasn't aware of the natural world because it was so fascinating. My father and I fished together and ate our catch with locally grown corn and melon bought at Rippey's farm stand. This experience is becoming more and more rare, removing people from that normal connection with the land and where their food comes from.*

You have a much more tenuous attachment to nature if you grow up in the city. I think that is why some people have a problem seeing the big picture because they weren't raised in the big picture. A recent science article in the New York Times *describes how we have removed ourselves so far from the environment that the environment no longer has a profound effect on us. We are no longer evolving in response to the environment.*

What disturbs me most about the state of the world today is humanity's tendency to elevate and separate society from nature. This view is accompanied by the notion that science and industry will always be able to remedy any problems that arise, from population growth to food production. In my mind, that is an elitist view that has little bearing on reality.

If I could accomplish the ultimate goal, it would be to bring organics to the mainstream and have consumers begin to see and understand its importance. There's much to be said for voting with your dollars. The more that consumers support sustainable agriculture, the more it will grow. If the organics industry continues its double-digit growth and continues the crossover to mainstream grocery stores, I'll feel like I've accomplished something.

"My little ritual is to spend as much time in nature as possible. I love to fish and hunt. I play in my garden and cook. And I meditate. This is what keeps me centered. As we all know, it's hard to find the time when you have a nine-to-five job. Although I mostly eat vegetables and grains, nothing tastes better to me than fresh-caught trout when I'm camping. I've also been known to eat a steak or two at Chez Pannisse in Berkeley, so I guess you could call me a flexitarian.

"I've also found that as I get older, I seem to lose sight of my goals if I don't get out in nature more. The time is much more rejuvenating. I also like to challenge myself to try new things, so recently I've started surfing. Floating in the water literally gives one a new perspective on life and teaches respect for the power of our birthplace, the ocean.

"Meditation is a fairly new endeavor for me, and is difficult to discuss because it is experiential. But it provides me with the excuse to just sit and breathe. It has taken me years to learn the importance of giving yourself the time to be quiet and enjoy a bit of personal time each day. If I can't find the time to get out and surf, or bike, I find it extremely restorative to have personal time for reflection."

MADELEINE L'ENGLE

Poet and author

"To attempt anything—music, love, art—is to risk failure, and that takes a kind of courage, I believe, to be uniquely feminine. This openness to change, interdependence, questions with no easy answers, vulnerability and risk is the feminine spirituality that is desperately needed if the human race is to reach the year 2000."

A s young girls, many of us sampled our first taste of mystical, other-dimensional worlds through Madeleine L'Engle's vivid science-fiction tale, *A Wrinkle in Time.* Following Mrs. Who, Mrs. Whatsit and Mrs. Which as they transcended space and time, we were launched on our own imaginative journeys into magical realms lying somewhere far, far away—or perhaps just beyond this visible world.

One of the most sage and spiritual writers of our time, L'Engle has written 44 books for children and adults, from *A Swiftly Tilting Planet* to *A Circle of Quiet.* All of her books speak of a sense of wonder in the mysterious, a perpetual awe in a universe that stretches out far beyond human comprehension, as she wrote in her book, *The Irrational Season.*

It was in this book that L'Engle shared her own first sensual experience of God one unusually clear and beautiful night on a stretch of beach in Florida. At the time, she was little more than a baby and was staying with her grandmother in an oceanside cottage. All she recalled of the visit was being picked up from her crib in what seemed the middle of the night and taken outdoors for her first look at the stars.

"I was intuitively aware not only of a beauty I had never seen before but also that the world was far greater than the protected limits of the small child's world, which was all that I had known thus far. . . .

"I had been taught to say my prayers at night: Our Father, and a long string of God-blesses, and it was that first showing of the galaxies that gave me an awareness that the God I spoke to at bedtime was extraordinary and not just a bigger and better combination of the grown-up powers of my mother and father."

This glimpse of glory, as she called it, was the first of other such epiphanies. Art, for instance, was a way to peer into the Divine for L'Engle as she grew up in a two-bedroom apartment near Central Park and the Metropolitan Museum of Art. "My parents had many friends in the arts. They were Episcopalians, and the Episcopal Church has always seen art as a way of worshipping God. I was a lonely child, so I also read a great deal. I read lots of 19th century English women writers whose faith was not explicit but implicit. I read myths, fairy tales, fantasies, but lived among people who had a rather open and strong faith."

L'Engle wrote her first story at the tender age of five. "I was very lucky. I knew very early that this was what I wanted to do and how I wanted to express myself."

L'Engle thinks the first seeds of her inner strength were planted during long hours of solitude as a young child. It was then she could open her gifts for daydreaming, storytelling and writing—even gardening, as it turned out.

When she was 12, L'Engle went to an English boarding school where the instructors taught the masculine values of stoicism, independence, obedience and bravery. She and the other students were given garden plots so they could grow produce for teatime. Instead, L'Engle used hers to sow poppies—nothing but poppies.

She had read that their opium induces beautiful dreams, so she supplied the students with poppy leaf, flower and seed sandwiches. At night she would take her flashlight and dream book to bed under her pillow and wait for the dreams to unspool.

From 1941 to 1947, L'Engle had an active theatrical career. It was in the theater that she met her husband, the actor Hugh Franklin. They eventually moved to her now famous Connecticut home, Crosswicks, where L'Engle raised a son and two daughters and found much of the experiences and inspiration for her books.

After 40 years of marriage, Hugh Franklin died in 1987 from cancer. L'Engle herself almost died from injuries from a car accident in 1991. "I have found that pain deepens our souls, our spiritual development. I do think this kind of pain is inevitable, for that is how we grow. Oysters make a pearl with the grit of sand, and the growth of our soul doesn't come free, either. There has to be some balance."

It was at Crosswicks that L'Engle first began to devour Albert Einstein's theories about time and time travel and Planck's quantum theory. Einstein's "beautiful theory" of a universe in which all things are interrelated in one field of energy fired L'Engle to write *A Wrinkle in Time*. The novel went on to win the prestigious Newbery Medal in 1963.

I was trying to write about a universe I could believe in because I was not finding the things I cared about in a logical place. Instead, they were in Einstein's theory of relativity and in quantum mechanics. Physicists, with their view of a connected universe, are really our modern-day mystics. This is the theology I study greatly.

I believe whatever we do not only affects ourselves but whomever we are in contact with, from our friends and neighbors to those we ride with on the subway. The butterfly effect is a favorite theory discussed among physicists. It says if a butterfly should fly into my office and somehow get hurt, the entire universe would feel it. Because everything is interconnected, the effect of the accident would be felt throughout the galaxy.

Because of the connectedness of life, there should be no separation between the spiritual and secular. We are both spiritual and material creatures at the same time. I had a brand new knee put in last winter. Since I was surrounded by love, concern and care, I healed incredibly well, way ahead of schedule.

What could have been a very unpleasant, totally painful experi-
ence was one of the most social winters I've had.

Women can uniquely reconcile the coexistence of pain and
pleasure, the spiritual and the secular, intellect and intuition, and
the tangible and mysterious nature of the universe. I think women
need to remember that we, unlike men, have been allowed to
remain in touch with the intuitive, the creative, the imaginative.
Men have often been forced by society to live by their reason. We
have been allowed a much fuller interior life, and we need to con-
tinue not only to develop that, but to share it.

I don't think we should shut ourselves off from the mysteri-
ous and the infinite. Look at the women who are now gaining a
lot of attention, like Teresa of Avila and Catherine of Sienna and
Hildegard of Bingen.

More people are definitely turning to the spiritual realm.
There is a dissatisfaction with the materialism that surrounds us
and does not make us happy. But a spiritual life has to be acted
out in the material world. Any other way won't work. If I am
thinking spiritually and deeply and have a spiritual relationship
with God, but I'm not nice to the person unloading groceries, it
won't work.

Living a more spiritual life can be as simple—yet as rich—as
joining together more often for good food, conversation and
fun. I think we need to laugh more often. We need to tell more
stories. We need to get together for dinner more often. Making
a meal can be a very spiritual activity. I like to sit around the
table talking until the candles burn down. That is one of my
favorite things to do. My granddaughters lived with me during
their college and postgraduate years, and living with them was
absolutely marvelous for me. We often got together for
evenings of good conversation, music, laughter and lovingness.

I live on the Upper West Side of New York, with a view of
sunsets over the Hudson River. One of my students said the
other day, "You know, my parents never see the sunset." We
need to see more sunsets.

We have a great longing for a sense of wonder and that's a
start. We also have to live in hope. The world has always been

in desperate situations. If we live in hope and are stubborn, have a sense of humor and hang in there, we will get through. Women must begin to increasingly conclude that they can and have to change the world themselves.

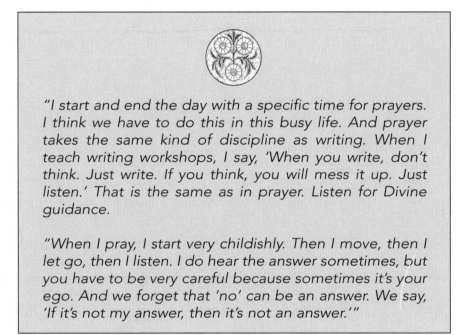

"I start and end the day with a specific time for prayers. I think we have to do this in this busy life. And prayer takes the same kind of discipline as writing. When I teach writing workshops, I say, 'When you write, don't think. Just write. If you think, you will mess it up. Just listen.' That is the same as in prayer. Listen for Divine guidance.

"When I pray, I start very childishly. Then I move, then I let go, then I listen. I do hear the answer sometimes, but you have to be very careful because sometimes it's your ego. And we forget that 'no' can be an answer. We say, 'If it's not my answer, then it's not an answer.'"

RACHEL NAOMI REMEN, M.D.

Founder and director, Institute for the
Study of Health and Illness, medical
director and cofounder of the
Commonweal Cancer Help Program
in California, and author

> *O*
> *Body*
> *for 35 years*
> *1,573 experts with*
> *14,372 combined years of training*
> *have failed*
> *to*
> *cure your wounds.*
> *Deep inside*
> *I*
> *am*
> *whole.*

D r. Rachel Naomi Remen has a 40-year history of life-threatening illness and has personally faced surgery seven times. Her work, then, is an intimate weaving of the perspectives of the patient and the physician, and she is deeply familiar with the emotions and needs of those facing death. When she was first ill in her teens, she reacted as many of us do to being thwarted and limited by illness.

"I was angry for years," she now laughs. "I hated all the others who were well." But one day while walking on a beach, she had a revelation in which she realized that in the vitality of her anger was her love of life and her wish to participate in life. After that her view of everything became different, and her anger was healed. She says she never looked back.

Dr. Remen now is the medical director and cofounder of the Commonweal Cancer Help Program in California, which was featured on the Bill Moyers' PBS program, "Healing and the Mind." She is also the founder and director of the Institute for the Study of Health and Illness, a training program for physicians who care for those with life-threatening illnesses. An assistant clinical professor of Family and Community Medicine at the University of California, San Francisco, School of Medicine, Dr. Remen teaches a course called "The Care of the Soul."

The experience of Spirit is central to her life and work, Dr. Remen says. "A deep sense of the spiritual leads one to trust not one's own lonely power but the great flow or pattern manifested in all life, including our own." For many years she has helped others, including patients and physicians, recognize the experience of the sacred in their daily lives and work. She believes we often fail to see the powerful impact that Spirit has on our lives, relationships and health. She remembers a moment in her career when she and her medical colleagues failed to see the mysterious when it was right in front of them.

"As a resident physician at Sloan-Kettering Cancer Hospital in New York, I worked with a patient whose X-rays showed a widespread metastatic cancer of the bone and lungs. He had tumors in his lungs and bones and was way beyond treatment. He was dying."

But in the two weeks the patient spent in the hospital without any treatment, his cancer went away and never came back. "Amazingly, we came to the conclusion that the chemotherapy he had finished nine months ago had finally worked. We did not recognize this example of The Mystery in any way. We were not awed. You can only see what you have grown an eye to see. Our medical system is the only system in human history that does not admit the possibility of Divine intervention."

Like those well-meaning doctors, we have all forgotten how to see everyday life as sacred, Dr. Remen explains.

This is not a society that respects subjective experience and the sacred and other ineffable experiences. This is a culture that values objective reality, that even attributes our healing to it. Things that are quantifiable, measurable and explainable are valued more than things that are inexplicable.

We have accepted the values of technology as our values, as the greater good in our society. If a life is useful and productive, it is a good life. These values will not satisfy human beings. We need something more meaningful than this to live well.

I hope to initiate a kind of questioning of the role of spirit in health, in health care and in life. Sacred experience is an essential need of human nature. Something in us all hungers for the sacred. And there is also something in each of us that is able to recognize the sacred when we encounter it, even if we are not able to describe it in words. We each do this in our own way.

I am a former pediatrician, and I know children have many experiences of the sacred. Many young children have told me about the angels or guardians that they see watching over them in the hospital. One little boy spoke often to his dead father, who he was convinced was sitting on the edge of his bed and helping him heal his broken leg. Often children are told, "That didn't really happen," which is confusing to them. Eventually they stop seeing the world around them. We need to develop our natural capacity to see and appreciate the sacred world around us. In the words of the poet Yeats, "The voyage of discovery lies not in seeking new vistas but in having new eyes."

Spirituality, then, is just about an awareness of the world and daily life. Even picking out a container of milk at the store is a spiritual decision. It is very possible to be aware of the gift and abundance of that container of milk and the people who have collaborated to make it possible for you to have it. We need to pay the same careful, meticulous attention to our inner reality that we have learned to pay to the details of our external lives.

It is possible to talk to someone who has chosen carefully every sofa cushion, every pair of stockings and every lipstick, and yet who still does not have a sense of the meaning of her life. If we could pay that same kind of careful attention to our inner world, we would come a lot closer to living well. There is nothing more that we need to do to experience the sacred—we just need to remember. The sacred experience is our human birthright.

It is such a universal capacity. Every culture in the world has a name for it. We call it the soul. Our souls are our capacity to experience the sacred. To do this, we do not have to be different or even more; we just need to remember who we are.

I am amused by the efforts to prove the reality of sacred experience. It is as if we are trying to prove the soul to the mind. Some things cannot be proved, but can be directly experienced. And the experience of such things can alter a life. In a funny way, we ask the smaller world to validate the larger realities, and you cannot do that. There are many things we cannot prove, but we can know and feel their power. Like love.

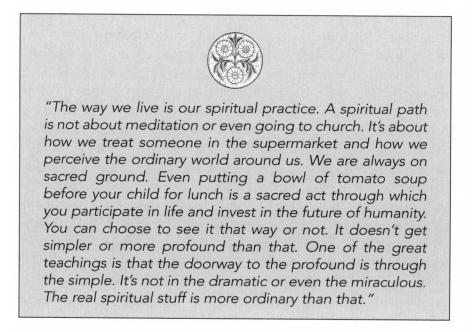

"The way we live is our spiritual practice. A spiritual path is not about meditation or even going to church. It's about how we treat someone in the supermarket and how we perceive the ordinary world around us. We are always on sacred ground. Even putting a bowl of tomato soup before your child for lunch is a sacred act through which you participate in life and invest in the future of humanity. You can choose to see it that way or not. It doesn't get simpler or more profound than that. One of the great teachings is that the doorway to the profound is through the simple. It's not in the dramatic or even the miraculous. The real spiritual stuff is more ordinary than that."

ADA DEER

Senior-level policy official,
Washington, D.C.

"I would like everyone to be a complete human by recognizing each other's humanity across the globe. It would mean peace, justice and equality."

S eason flowing into season, Ada Deer came of age in a one-room cabin on the banks of Wisconsin's Wolf River. "We would hear the geese flying over and the river breaking through the ice in the spring, bringing the heavy rush of water. We saw squirrels and occasionally deer in the fields. This was my early orientation to the world's life."

As the earth's rhythms transformed the land around her, her internal view changed as well. A member of Wisconsin's Menominee tribe, Deer knew her bonds with her people and the land compelled her to follow an inner calling to restore Native American heritages. "My mother always told me, 'You are not on this planet for your own pleasures, but to help people. You are an Indian, and your duty and responsibility is to help Indians, your tribe and all others.' I will be 60, and I am still working on my mother's agenda."

Deer's mother, Connie, was the daughter of a Philadelphia minister. An extremely independent, nonconformist young woman, she chose to become a public-health nurse and postpone marriage. She eventually worked in Appalachia, South Dakota's Rosebud Sioux Reservation and finally in Wisconsin, where she met Joe Deer, Ada's father. "I have this zeal, instilled in me by my mother, to help others—especially as I learn more about our society and the causes and effects of poverty and racism. My mother taught me to think, question and be my own person. That's a very valuable lesson that has stood me well through my entire life."

Her mother's support and her own determination to make a better life for herself propelled Deer to some of the highest achievements ever realized by an American Indian. She became the first chairwoman of her tribe and the first in her tribe to graduate from the University of Wisconsin. She later received her master's in social work from Columbia University. "I was drawn to social work because it embodies many Indian values and is dedicated to social justice and the elimination of discrimination."

After college, Deer's activism unfolded purposefully. She was a founding board member of Americans for Indian Opportunity and Independent Sector. She was a Common Cause board member and helped recruit the first American Indians for service to the Peace Corps. Appointed by the Senate to the American Indian Policy Review Commission, she chaired the National Support Committee of the Native American Rights Fund. She was appointed by Presidents Carter and Reagan to the President's Commission on White House Fellowships.

In 1972, she became the first Indian to successfully lobby Congress to restore tribal rights, and the Menominee Restoration Act was signed into law in 1973, leading the way for other tribes to restore federal recognition.

Twenty years later, Deer became the first American Indian woman to run for Congress in Wisconsin. Now a senior-level policymaker in Washington, D.C., Deer says her work to bring more social justice and equity to Native American people around the country is imprinted with a sense of connectedness to and compassion for all people.

"One has to feel a connection to all humanity and to the entire universe. In our dominant society today, everything is too fragmented, and we are all too compartmentalized, segmented and ultimately alienated from one another. I don't feel that way. I feel a connection to everyone and everything."

When Deer runs into obstacles in her efforts to bring about

more social and economic equality for American Indians, she sometimes recalls—in addition to her mother's words—those of another nonconformist—Eleanor Roosevelt, with whom she spent an afternoon in 1956.

I was with a group of young people from The Encampment for Citizenship who spent the afternoon with Eleanor Roosevelt at Hyde Park. I was impressed by the fact that here was the former First Lady taking time out to open up her home to talk to a group of young students. There was not much in it for her.

Well, I was never a shy person, so when I had a chance to ask Eleanor Roosevelt a question, I did. The United Nations had just been formed, and Mrs. Roosevelt was involved in the UN Commission on Human Rights. So I asked her about South Africa. How could South Africa be a member of the UN and treat Black people so terribly, and what could the UN do about it? Why didn't they just throw South Africa out?

And Eleanor Roosevelt didn't say, "Well, that was a stupid question." What she said was, "That is a very good question. But you have to understand that violence is not the way to solve human problems. Education is, and it takes time and patience for people to go through the educational process." Now, from time to time, when I get angry during some of my activities, I remember what she said. Solving problems is difficult. And it does take a lot of hard work and patience.

It also takes a lot of work to be a spiritual person if you are going to be honest about it and not just go through the motions of going to church and what I consider other superficial aspects of being religious. First you have to feel within yourself your own power, your spiritual, moral and physical strength. I don't think enough people today strive for and work at that. I do that as much as I can. And at 60, I like myself. I can say, "Yea, I made a difference. I wasn't just breathing and taking up space on the planet."

Know thyself. That is a continuous journey as we progress through life. By this I mean: understand and accept your own humanity, and appreciate your strengths and weaknesses, and continually strive.

Basically, we are all a product of our families, communities and culture. If you study your family history and your background, you can accept your heritage. I don't know everything I would like to know about my Menominee background or about my mother's English, Scottish and Irish side. But I recently visited with a 93-year-old friend of my mother's twin sister and she reminded me of my Quaker background. I really believe that what the Quakers have done and practice is needed on a larger scale. Their basic belief is that God is within each person.

On my mother's side, we are related in a very distant way to Francis Bacon. Ultimately, everyone here on planet Earth should feel connected. I like Chief Seattle's speech because it expresses the world view of many American Indians. It expresses very eloquently our connection to humans, water, plants, animals and all life.

Maintaining these connections helps me stay balanced and focused. I go out to Indian country and see the little children, the land and the animals. I just came back from Alaska and was with a native person who is probably out right now whaling. That was a very direct connection for me, to see how important the whaling is for his tribe's identity and culture.

You are continually receptive to these connections if you live your life with open ears, open eyes and an open heart. I find it very enriching, comforting, sustaining and energizing to feel the connections. I love people. I feel we are all here on this planet together. We all have to work not just to survive, but to make it better for the coming generations. I have two brothers and two sisters, lots of nieces and nephews, and through these innocent little eyes looking up at you, you see the future generations. Indians say that what you do today affects seven future generations. That's not what the dominant society accepts. We must think most of all about the future of our young people.

On this night, tens of thousands of girls and boys across

Indian country will go to sleep. Some in my Wisconsin homeland will hear the vibrant sounds I heard many years ago in the cabin where I grew up. Others will hear the wind in the Douglas fir trees at Warm Springs, the surging current of the great Missouri at Fort Peck or the song of the canyon wren calling out from a redrock monument at Navajo. There is no reason why all these children cannot grow up to live in prosperity, in good health, with excellent educations, in clean environments and immersed in their rich traditions.

"I have a very strong passion for art because art is a universal language. In my office I have baskets, carvings, paintings and other art from various tribal groups. If I take time to contemplate them, which I do, I think what a beautiful vision these artists have. On my window I am looking at a Winnebago ash basket presented to me in Wisconsin. I know many Winnebagos, so this basket brings forth memories of them. Next to that is a beautiful poem by a Navajo. Next to that is a drum by the Muckleshoot Tribe in Washington. Then I have a basket in the shape of a canoe given to me by a friend.

"This beauty around me reminds me of the creativity of all human beings. It evokes good thoughts and emotions. It's very powerful."

ARDATH RODALE

Chairman and chief executive officer,
Rodale Press, and author

"Strength to climb toward the light does not come easily. It requires opening yourself up to all the tides, one wave at a time. Eventually you get strong enough to withstand life's elements. Is it worth the struggle? Without a doubt."

W hen she was a teenager, Ardath Rodale—born in a hurry in 1928—wrote that she wished her soul would always have mountains so high she could never scale them. That imaginative spirit has allowed her to climb toward something greater than herself, even as her journey plunged her into some of life's loneliest valleys.

Rodale is chairman and chief executive officer of Rodale Press and Rodale Institute, two of the most influential publishing and nonprofit organizations in the country. Rodale Press publishes *Prevention*, *Men's Health*, *Organic Gardening*, *Bicycling*, *Runner's World* and *Backpacker*, among other titles.

But what Rodale may be most known for is her ability to gracefully and courageously glean lessons from life's harshest moments. "I believe the reason we're here on earth is to help other people, to make the world a better place, to keep it safe and to grow in understanding of one another. My husband always used the word, 'Regenerate.' Well, the time has come for us to look at our lives and say, 'We need to regenerate, renew and restore the land instead of using the land and everything that surrounds us; otherwise we're not going to have it.'"

In the late 1960s, Rodale and her husband, Robert, launched their mission to regenerate the land. They bought hundreds of acres near Kutztown, Pennsylvania, and turned the site into the

Rodale Institute, an international research center for organic farming and sustainable agriculture. Institute staff now work in developing countries, from Senegal to Guatemala, sharing practical information on sustainable agriculture.

Tragically, just as he was spreading the institute's mission even further, Robert Rodale was killed in a car accident in Russia. He was returning home after successfully setting up a joint venture to work with Russian farmers.

Even after losing her husband, Rodale says his presence still sustains her as she carries out possibly her most important work—opening hearts and minds to those suffering from AIDS. In 1985, after being ill only five days, the Rodales' son, David, died from complications due to AIDS. He was diagnosed only two days before. "The hardest experience to face in life is the death of a child. But in my heart, I kept hearing David urging me, 'Mom, you have a story to tell. Please help people understand.'"

In 1989, Rodale wrote *Climbing Toward the Light—A Journey of Growth, Understanding and Love* to explain how her family's love and faith carried them through their loss of David. She has since become one of the first to share with groups all over the country the story of AIDS from a personal viewpoint. "I think my greatest gift in life has been my opening myself up to share our lives and help other people."

Just as she was about to embark on a tour for her book, Rodale was diagnosed with cancer. It was then that she discovered the wisdom in nurturing and rejuvenating herself, just as she had the land and those around her.

Her illness, she now sees, was a "gentle nudge" that helped her learn she could accept others' support and in turn, help others diagnosed with cancer. "I discovered a whole new dimension of reaching out to others, receiving their love and concern and then sharing with people to help them face similar experiences."

A sought-after speaker, Rodale has given workshops on AIDS at the National Conference for Compassionate Friends and is an honorary mother for Mothers' Voices Against AIDS. In 1994, she received an Honorary Doctorate of Humane Letters from Allentown College of St. Francis De Sales in Pennsylvania, and in 1995, Rodale received a Doctor of Laws degree from Kutztown University, her alma mater.

When she most needs solace and strength, her husband still communicates his love and pride in her, often through a message from the natural world, Rodale says.

It happens at very important times of my life, when a particularly beautiful experience in nature corresponds with my need for being uplifted in my own life. The first time this happened, I thought it might be an accident. But when it keeps happening, you say, "Well, no, this couldn't be an accident. It's happening too often."

Soon after Bob's death, when I was particularly sad and needing to be comforted, I woke in the middle of the night and wondered why the room was so bright. A brilliant large full moon was shining like a halo around a stained glass butterfly that hung in the window. How is it that I woke at that particular moment? Since then, it has happened several more times.

Another time, when I was feeling really sad about Bob and I just wanted to share some great experience that had happened, I came into the bedroom and the sun was hitting a prism on the windowsill. There were rainbows dancing all around the room. Right over Bob's bed, they shone down like a star.

Still another fantastic experience I had concerning Bob took place when I shared David's story with those attending the Northeastern Lutheran Synod Convention, to help them understand the tragedy of AIDS and the need for their unconditional love to shine as children of God. I was hoping that the Lutherans would open their hearts wider and be more understanding of people who have AIDS. It was a tremendous experience. There were more than 1,000 people in the audience and it was perhaps one of the very best speeches I ever gave.

As I was driving home, the sun shining in my face, I looked in the rearview mirror and there I saw Bob's face smiling as if he was walking in back of the car. At the same time there was a song playing on the radio, "There's someone walking behind you, turn around, look at me." The tears just streamed down my face and I knew he was really proud of me. That face will never leave my mind.

To the American Indians, feathers have spiritual significance. Lately these appear at my feet when I am on special contemplation walks, and I feel a closeness to Bob. His love still surrounds me.

My experiences have taught me that we need to remember that we all experience losses in life, whether a divorce, loss of a job, alienation of family members or death itself. Each loss has a grieving process that needs to be dealt with. None of these can be treated lightly, and sometimes the healing takes a long time. After my husband was killed, I was in utter disbelief. Sometimes we are numb, sometimes we are hurt, and other times we are filled with anger.

One day after Bob was gone, I said to my son, Anthony, that I wondered why I didn't feel any emotion. He said to me, "Mom, you need a counselor. If I hadn't been seeing a counselor when Dad died, I wouldn't have made it." I did go to a counselor. She told me that I had had too much in my life in a short period and that not feeling was nature's way of giving me only what I could handle at the time. She said that as I got stronger, the feeling would return, and it has.

I found a book, Songs from the Edge—Memoirs and Poetry, by Fay Harden. In it, she writes, "The colors of life change as we go through grief. We begin black and white, then grey settles over us, seeping into our pores, smothering us for a period of time, then slowly, the colors change, we may not even be aware of their changing, till one day we see a rainbow and know it was meant for us."

While we work through the black and white and grey of our lives to reach that rainbow, we need to get rid of the stress we face. Time for ourselves is often at the end of our priority lists. I can pinpoint in my own life the mega-stress before the onset of any illness I have faced. Sometimes we aren't even aware that our bodies are a taut vine from situations in life we haven't come to terms with.

How we respond mentally, emotionally and spiritually affects our bodies. Our bodies are like tuning forks. They carry the pitch but are not the source of the vibration. How we translate life's challenges into our emotions and how we express those emotions determine whether we vibrate freely and easily or whether we block up. Just walking is a natural tranquilizer, but we need to fill the experience with real pleasure to keep it interesting. My urgent request is that you take the time while walking to look around and see what is there. Smell the fragrances, hear the birds, feel the elements of nature. Bring them into your mind so that you can call upon those feelings as the day wears on and when you get caught up in too much. Take minute fantasies to travel back to those special moments to relive your feelings of peace and joy.

I have become involved in doing discovery walks with children at our farm. In planning the walks, I only thought of finding and tasting fruits and vegetables. The children thought to investigate locust shells, butterflies, grasshoppers and Indian stones. I became enriched with smiles, the joy of seeing strawberry-smudged faces, the hugs, no thought of time and wandering in open spaces wherever imagination and creativity could be found.

I urge you to try it if you want to recapture the free child that you once were. Let go of the stress. Take time in your busy world to quiet the mind. We can become rich beyond measure if we once again feel the amazement of simple things and follow on a new life of exciting adventure.

"My definition of spirituality is easy. I feel it's the unity of the mind, body and spirit, altogether and unified in one body. It's simple. Twenty years ago, listening to a college symphony, I felt through the music the importance of harmony for mind, body and spirit, and I have been trying very hard to bring a peaceful harmony into my life ever since.

"I think one of the main things we need to do is take time to be alone. I read a lot of inspirational books that help me expand my mind as far as my spiritual life and my surroundings in nature. When I'm finished with my exercise program in the morning, I really love to do affirmations for health and love. And then I do affirmations for beauty, good business and love.

"In the evening, I make a thankful list for certain people in my life with whom I shared an experience in the day. It's kind of like an opening and closing of the day. And I hug trees—I had to feel a couple until I found one that really gave me energy. Another thing I enjoy is my swing. Some days, when I just feel like I need a change, I go and sit in the swing and watch the clouds. And my dog jumps up and sits with me, and we swing together!"

MARILYN FERGUSON

Human potential consultant, editor of
the *Brain/Mind Bulletin* and author

*"We each have a kind of inner prompting that will say,
'Bring an umbrella,' even if it's a sunny day. If you over-
rationalize, question and negate that intuitive feeling,
you miss the point."*

Millions of people, Marilyn Ferguson wrote in 1980, were discovering their capacity for endless awakenings in a universe of endless surprises. She had no idea how many millions. Her groundbreaking book, *The Aquarian Conspiracy: Personal and Social Transformation in Our Time*, tapped such a sensitive chord in society's collective consciousness that it has since been translated into a dozen languages.

"There were many more of us across the far-flung reaches of the earth than I ever imagined. I had more allies who were sensing a dramatic change in our larger society than I ever thought were there."

Ferguson's classic message is even more germane today, appealing to each of us to awaken to our inner strengths, to transform society from the inside out and to follow our intuition in challenging the status quo in every realm, from science to the arts.

Ferguson first discovered her intuitive nature as a young girl. "I had a sense of the mystical from childhood on. When I was a small child, I heard voices. I used to talk about beings under the ground until I was about four. My cousin thought we were pretending, so I was embarrassed because I wasn't pretending. From then on, the mystical tendencies I had were most expressed in church.

"When my daughter, Kris, was six, she confided that she

heard voices. I think a lot of adults forget they had these experiences."

One day in 1968, Ferguson was home by herself in California when she heard a voice call her name twice. "There was no one around. I wondered if it might have something to do with a family member. I thought of my brother, but he had just returned from Vietnam, and I knew he was safe.

"I went out on an errand. When I returned, my husband was waiting to tell me that my father had died. When I went to Colorado for his funeral, I learned that my former husband and my cousin in New York had premonitions about my father's death. Other phenomena had also occurred.

"This made me think there must be many things happening that people aren't talking about."

The experience dramatically escalated her explorations into consciousness. Later, when Ferguson began to practice Transcendental Meditation, she had further direct experiences that confirmed her sense of the mystical. "It was the experience of becoming pure electricity, of experiencing the self that never dies. It somehow confirmed something I had taken on faith in my Lutheran upbringing—the boundless realm behind the material world."

Ferguson's experiences with meditation, psychic phenomena and her young children drew her to investigate psychological and physiological phenomena. Already a published author and poet, Ferguson embarked on an avid exploration of brain research. In 1973, she published *The Brain Revolution*, a survey of new scientific insights into that most complex organ. Two years later, she launched *Brain/Mind Bulletin*, a Los Angeles-based international newsletter tracking psychology, neuroscience, states of consciousness, meditation, learning and related topics.

Long a sought-after speaker, Ferguson has shared her insights with diverse groups. Then Senator Al Gore twice invited her to address the Congressional Clearinghouse on the Future, which he cofounded. Her addresses to corporations like Hallmark and IBM are intended to stimulate creativity in leaders and to catalyze the power of those who have never thought of themselves as creative. Ferguson is currently completing a new book, *Radical Common Sense*, which draws heavily on the traits and methods of leading visionaries.

Ferguson believes each of us was born a visionary. We simply must learn to access our inherent powers, unique strengths and creativity.

We just need to identify a purpose that inspires us to get up in the morning. The visionaries of history saw something that needed doing, and their purpose then became unifying.

When you learn to hear and heed your inner direction—whether it's a vision, a voice or a gut feeling—your hunches grow stronger. We sometimes feel mysteriously prompted to take a particular road, go to a certain store or call someone. Sometimes when I'm speaking in public, I'm moved to relate a certain anecdote, for example, and it often turns out to address someone's specific need.

The process of finding a project begins by applying the art of noticing. Spend a week or two making notes on everything you see that needs help in your neighborhood or in the larger community. Then look at your list and see what's most compelling. It might be something as local as getting a gate at a dangerous railroad crossing. Let that be your cause.

Check out your hunches. I didn't want to publish Brain/Mind Bulletin, *for example, but I had a series of dreams about cars. I realized I was being shown that the publication would be a "vehicle" for the issues that interested me.*

Our society is falling apart largely because we are too intent on our own plans and ambitions. We need the sense of adventure that comes from living a visionary life. We must come to realize that talking to an aging parent or helping a neighbor's child may be more important than our original agenda.

"Even those at the frontiers of science emphasize that the future is uncertain. Developing our intuitive capacity is a solid, practical step."

FRANCES VAUGHAN

Psychologist and author

"Remembering our dreams is often an empowering process. When we acknowledge dreams as inner resources available to us all the time, we can tap into a deep source of inner wisdom and resilience."

Mohammed said he received a message of his mission through a dream. Buddha's birth was announced to his mother in a dream. In the Bible, many of the prophets heard God's voice as they slept. Virtually every spiritual tradition makes some reference to the power of dreams as a gateway to our subconscious—and a doorway to the Divine.

Dreams, says author and psychologist Frances Vaughan, are not only an invaluable source of guidance on the spiritual path; they can lead to enhanced healing, creativity and wisdom. "Dreams are very useful, and I have noticed that when people reflect on them in a spiritual context, dreams can be helpful for spiritual growth and development.

"If there is something going on in the psyche that deserves attention, for instance, it will often surface in our dreams. Self-deception is much easier in our waking life. Dreams can call attention to unfinished business or issues we need to address."

For 25 years, Vaughan has been a highly valued pioneer in the transpersonal psychology movement. A longtime student of Zen, she has helped psychologists worldwide bridge the gap between spirituality and science. Formerly on the clinical faculty at the University of California, College of Medicine, at Irvine, Vaughan is a past president of the Association for Transpersonal Psychology and has lectured on transpersonal psychology around the world. She has written *Awakening Intuition*, *Shadows of the Sacred* and *The Inward Arc*. With her husband, Roger Walsh, she coedited several books, including *Paths Beyond Ego*. In her books, Vaughan illustrates how the world of dreams and illusions can yield a wealth of clinical material about someone's pain, pleasures and intimate needs. She points to her own dreams that involve traveling along roads, with varying degrees of difficulty.

One such personal dream she related in her book, *The Inward Arc*. She recalls from the dream that she was riding a bike with difficulty along a "muddy, rutted road," trying to avoid all sorts of obstacles. She remembers to shift her attention and not concentrate solely on the road. She realizes if she just keeps pedaling she will be all right.

Then she notices someone riding beside her and if they pedal in synch, the pedaling is rhythmic, easier and more enjoyable: "Suddenly we are lifted off the ground and are riding through the air, quite effortlessly. I feel a strong humming vibration that seems to connect us as we continue riding joyously above the ground.

"The dream helped me realize that life seems easier when we don't think we have to do everything alone, but sometimes it takes effort and courage to keep going."

Dreams can deliver many reassuring messages, if we only heed them, Vaughan says.

We need to remember that dreams have historically been a source of wisdom through the ages in many religions. Some of the founders of the great traditions received messages in their dreams.

Sometimes spiritual teachings can come through our dreams. Many people, for example, experience visiting their teachers in their dreams. Some experience initiation dreams with their teachers. Recently, a woman told me of an experience that happened to her at the threshold between dreaming and waking.

This woman had a guru who was very important to her, and one night about 3:00 A.M., she awakened and experienced his presence in the room. She believed she wasn't really dreaming, even though it felt like a dream. She seemed to be in some other dimension and she was listening to spiritual beings having a conversation about being in form.

The message was that when human beings come into form, they don't like the limitations of being in their bodies. Everyone complains about being in this body: "If only my body were taller or shorter or lighter or darker." Everyone complains that her form won't change and feels stuck with a particular body. This causes a great deal of suffering because we don't like to accept our physical limitations. Later, when our bodies change as we age and approach death, we get upset because our forms are changing. Unfortunately, we aren't happy either way—when change seems impossible or when it seems inevitable. It's too bad human beings don't just accept what it's like to be in form.

When she heard the message in a semidream state, she thought she should get up and write it all down. "This is an important message because I have always struggled with my weight," she thought. Then she heard another message. "Don't worry. You will remember. You don't need to write it down." So she went back to sleep. At 5:00 A.M. she received a telephone call that her guru had died at 3:00 A.M.

This is just one example of the experiences that happen often in dreams or states of reverie. Clients have often told me of similar experiences in which they seem to feel the presence of loved ones who are far away or who have died. When we are dreaming or in a very quiet, relaxed state of consciousness, we seem to be more receptive and open.

In spiritual practice, we sometimes neglect the threshold between dreaming and waking. In ancient Greece, people would go to the Temple of Asclepius and ask for a healing dream. And the god of healing was said to appear in dreams to tell them what was needed for healing. I think we can avail ourselves of dreams for healing more than we usually do. In working with people as a therapist, I find that when they are in touch with and bring their dreams into therapy, they open a doorway into the unconscious and provide valuable guidance for what is needed for healing.

I myself have had several dreams of initiation. I remember one in which I received a transmission and a blessing from a guru I didn't particularly like and of whom I had been critical. In my dream, he came to me and put his hands on my head, and I experienced a tremendous flow of energy. This enabled me to let go of some of my judgments about him. I was able to be more detached and accept the teaching he offered at the level he was teaching. I think it also helped me lighten up some of my judgments about other people and recognize that we each have only a little piece of the puzzle. Each of us can speak to some people. I am grateful that many people are doing valuable work that I could not do. That dream was helpful to me.

By paying attention to our dreams, we also develop our intuition. As we listen to our dreams, we learn to listen to the deeper part of ourselves that we're out of touch with in our ordinary waking state. We have to believe our dreams are important if we want them to be helpful. You can practice talking to your dreams and say, "Dreams, I want to remember you. Will you be more accessible?" Making an effort to pray and ask for guidance within your dreams can be very fruitful. If you are a meditator and remember to sit down and meditate in your dream, it can be very interesting.

Why have we turned away from this understanding of spiritual guidance in dreams? Living in a materialistic culture, we are just beginning to reclaim some of the subjective spiritual experiences that have been missing from our culture. We have found that higher levels of material prosperity don't necessarily make us any happier. Since many of us have the good fortune to live in a culture that enables us to have the things we need, we want more in life than fulfillment of basic needs. Many of us have been suffering from a sense of spiritual deprivation.

Now, as some old forms and institutions are disintegrating, new forms of spirituality are emerging. We have access to many of the world's spiritual teachings that were not available 50 years *ago—a tremendously rich source of information. People are discovering a sense of spiritual renewal. I see a widespread grassroots movement exploring new forms of spirituality and I think that's very encouraging.*

There have always been people who were dissatisfied with traditional forms of religious practice and who had a longing for a sense of spiritual well-being. Now I think there is more appreciation of the fact that spirituality is not the property of any one particular religion. Spirituality is something that exists in the hearts and minds of men and women everywhere, both within and outside of traditions.

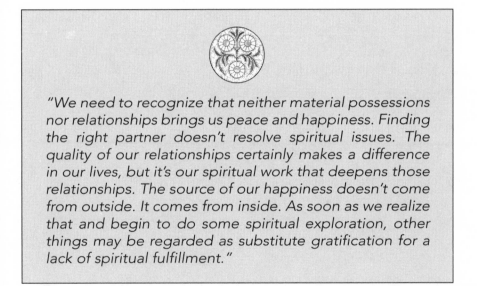

"We need to recognize that neither material possessions nor relationships brings us peace and happiness. Finding the right partner doesn't resolve spiritual issues. The quality of our relationships certainly makes a difference in our lives, but it's our spiritual work that deepens those relationships. The source of our happiness doesn't come from outside. It comes from inside. As soon as we realize that and begin to do some spiritual exploration, other things may be regarded as substitute gratification for a lack of spiritual fulfillment."

JOAN HALIFAX

Medical anthropologist, author, cultural
ecologist, Buddhist teacher and
founder of Upaya, a Buddhist center
in New Mexico

*"I try to bring to my relationships with the dying mind-
fulness and compassion. These relationships have had
a profound effect on my own life. I have learned more
helping others to face death than in doing anything
else in my life."*

From the 1960s to the 1980s, Joan Halifax ventured into
many corners of life in her quest for a raw, personal connection with truth. A medical anthropologist, she has spent time
with native peoples in Africa, Asia and Mexico, crossed the
Sahara, and studied trance states in Morocco.

After she participated with patients dying of cancer in LSD
experiments conducted by her former husband, psychiatrist
Stanislav Grof, Halifax hit rock bottom, psychologically, physically and spiritually. "I was very enthusiastic about learning
about the nature of consciousness, and it got me in a lot of trouble. I should have been content with simpler things," she says
20 years later.

Halifax eventually turned to Buddhist practice as "the ballast
that kept my ship upright." Her root teacher is Vietnamese Zen
monk Thich Nhat Hanh, one of the West's most respected
teachers of Buddhism. Halifax received the Lamp Transmission
in 1990 and is ordained to teach Buddhism. "Without Buddhism
and the practice of stability, I could have easily died in some of
the landscapes I entered years ago."

From 1976 to 1979, Halifax helped mythologist Joseph
Campbell assemble his atlas *Way of the Animal Powers*. At the
time, she continued to visit indigenous peoples in Mexico to
study shamanism and the psychoactive properties of plants like
peyote.

One morning Halifax told Campbell about a dream she'd had in which she was in a longhouse of the native peoples of Canada. Outside there was a great circle of men and women from all the nations standing in a green meadow. As she walked toward them, she started rising in the air. Soon others levitated with her and she awoke ecstatic.

When she related the dream to Campbell, he remarked wryly, "Joan, you should put pennies in your shoes." Campbell was right, she concluded. She needed to be more grounded. Continuously drawn to the "big views of the mountains," in 1979 Halifax established the Ojai Foundation in California, an educational center that merged Buddhism and shamanism.

Since 1990, she has been the President of Upaya, a Buddhist center in Sante Fe, New Mexico. In 1994, Upaya created The Project on Being With Dying, to give dying people and their caregivers more spiritual and practical support. The program helps ease their suffering, alienation and loneliness through contemplative practices such as mindfulness, meditation, prayer and other devotional practices.

Halifax is the author of *The Human Encounter with Death* (with Stanislav Grof), *Shamanic Voices*, *Shaman: The Wounded Healer* and *The Fruitful Darkness: Reconnecting with the Body of the Earth*. She has been on the faculty of Columbia University, the University of Miami School of Medicine, the New School for Social Research, the Naropa Institute and the California Institute of Integral Studies. Her various academic awards include a National Science Foundation Fellowship in Visual Anthropology and an appointment as an Honorary Research Fellow of Medical Ethnobotany at Harvard University's Peabody Museum.

In spite of Halifax's rigorous pursuit of the connections that bind us all—creatures, plants and humans alike—she doesn't regard her life as in any way unique.

You know I eat oatmeal in the morning, wash the dishes and do what everyone else does. There are just a few more things.

Some of my life people might find unusual, but I think if they tried it they might find it usual. I think a person who lives a spiritual life doesn't think about living a spiritual life. You just do what you have to do. There is nothing else you can do but this.

But asking people to do more, try harder, strive and go beyond what they are already doing sounds exhausting. It's more about opening ourselves, accepting, releasing and surrendering. It is about coming more fully into what is exactly here. Life is here and death is here. And both are a way to enter into an "ultimate closeness" in our experience of relationships, whether it's a relationship with the so-called natural world or with an individual who is in a very critical moment of his or her life.

One leads a life like this to abide in ultimate closeness with all that is. Being in the natural world, the wilderness makes that sense of relatedness more visible. You look at your own life, and when you're with the dying, you realize that death is part of everything. Being with the dying closely means that you are willing to suffer the same way a dying person suffers.

I had not intended to widen the scope of my work with dying people. I was content to spend time with people with life-threatening illnesses in an informal way, as I have done for many years. But in the past several years, there has been a strong call in our community and other communities around the country to teach people how to bring a contemplative dimension to being with dying.

People want a peaceful death, a gentle death. We, each of us, want to die well. I would like to help a few people die in a distinguished way. I would like to be of service to those involved in caregiving and help them develop an inner posture so they can do their work in a more skillful and nourishing way. It has been a great privilege and challenge to be a kind of midwife to dying people.

The call that leads us to our life's work is not always one we can hear. It's felt behind the eyes. It's felt in the hand. It's not necessarily someone telling us, "I want you to do this." It's our response to something more ineffable, more intangible.

We are placed, or we find ourselves, or our road takes us to *where we are needed. Often we flail about and go on side courses, but those side courses often give more body to the main road, which we don't even know we are walking on.*

Actually, I don't think we're even walking on a road. What I think we are doing is laying down a path as we walk, as we go along. The path behind us disappears, and there is nothing in front of us.

It is more about being fully present. And being fully present with the dying can be a powerful experience. To sit there and not want to be somewhere else. There you are. We often don't allow ourselves to experience that. We are afraid to see death, to be with death.

Leo Tolstoy, in The Death of Ivan Iyich, *describes how Ivan Iyich dies. We, the readers, are inside of him as he meets death and realizes there is no death. That is an extraordinary insight on the part of Tolstoy—that death per se does not exist.*

My dharma name in Vietnamese is "Chan Tiep," which means "True Continuation." It was given to me by Thich Nhat Hanh on one of my birthdays. People came up to me and wished me a happy continuation day. I had to smile.

As I talk to you now, I am sitting here looking at the trees, clouds and mountains. I can see the connectedness of life and death, and there is a kind of joy in feeling a part of this. Yet, the more I understand the less I know. I have a feeling I really don't know very much.

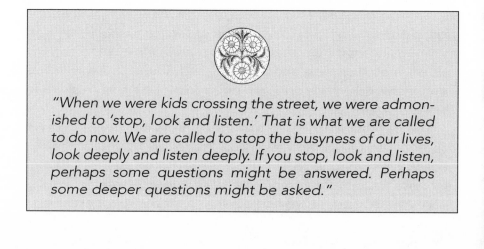

"When we were kids crossing the street, we were admonished to 'stop, look and listen.' That is what we are called to do now. We are called to stop the busyness of our lives, look deeply and listen deeply. If you stop, look and listen, perhaps some questions might be answered. Perhaps some deeper questions might be asked."

BONNIE STEINBERG

Spiritual leader, Temple Isaiah of
Great Neck, Long Island, New York

"I use the quilt analogy for my philosophy of how you piece your life together. Through these pieces of your life, you hope that somehow you will have a whole quilt. Usually you have a piece or two missing, but you act throughout the day to try to make it come together. It still may feel like patchwork, but eventually, you hope your life is more put together than fragmented."

In the early 1970s, Bonnie Steinberg was a college student at Lake Forest College near Chicago, studying to become an anthropologist. And then one of those seemingly chance encounters transformed her life forever. She enrolled in a class taught by now-popular author and theologian Larry Kushner, and anthropology became a stepping stone to her true path.

"Like many of us in the class, my Judaism was frozen at about an elementary school level. And religious concepts aren't easily translated to elementary school students. It takes an adult perspective and sensibility to come to them with any kind of creativity and meaning. For most of us, Kushner's class was the first time we had a real adult encounter with being Jewish and knowing Judaism."

The granddaughter of immigrants whose Judaism became fragmented as they settled in America, Steinberg feels her understanding of Judaism was always incomplete. "I had a real solid bedrock feeling about being Jewish, but there was little content to it. And I grew up in a very anti-Semitic suburb of Boston, so I had a lot to wrestle with. I had a really easy life in many ways. I had no medical challenges and I had very loving parents and a nice house. But I still had profound questions."

Studying with Kushner was the spark that lit her inner searchings, Steinberg recalls. Maybe, she thinks, the experience was what in Yiddish is called *bashert*, or a Divine coincidence, meant to happen. "I kept a notebook during that class and began to articulate what I felt. A kind of cynicism from the past began to fall away and was replaced by a much more hopeful and helpful way of thinking of one's Judaism. A year later, Kushner moved to Boston, so it was a privilege to have had that experience."

Her spiritual awakening under way, Steinberg decided to dedicate her life to being a Jewish anthropologist. "Then I realized I should really consider going to rabbinical school, so I transferred to Brandeis University." She was ordained in 1979. Steinberg, who regards herself as a liberal and a feminist, became the first female rabbi on Long Island. She is now the spiritual leader of Temple Isaiah of Great Neck.

She is also a regular essayist. In 1991, in the wake of extensive media coverage of the William Kennedy Smith trial and the Clarence Thomas hearings, she wrote a poignant and provocative piece in the *Long Island Jewish World*. The magnitude of the media attention focused on these trials, she wrote, shows how desperately our society is groping for a way to discuss ethics and morality.

"People are trying to find answers in all kinds of desperate ways. We cannot look to only one idea, person or institution for solutions. We need a variety of resources and voices and traditions to educate the human soul. . . .

"At the core, though, the answers are inside each one of us to love our neighbor as ourself, to do unto one's neighbor as one would have them do to us. It is that embarrassingly simple."

Because of her own struggle to come to terms with her beliefs, Steinberg can empathize with those who still feel cynical, disappointed or confused about their spirituality. "For too many people, old religious questions, rhetoric and rituals are frozen in time because they don't have the imagination or the life experiences to approach them with a fresh perspective."

Many things can awaken a visceral sense of the spiritual, Steinberg believes. A fuller aesthetic life that sharpens the senses can rekindle an appreciation of the spiritual mysteries of life, she explained in another essay.

"People love beauty and art, and using all of our senses is important to our religious experience. We love the natural beauty of the seashore or the country or the mountains. We travel to see special museums, artists' studios or the great religious spaces of the ages. Foreign or old synagogues and archeological sites have special meaning for us. Old churches and mosques intrigue us. New smells and sounds and colors tell us we are somewhere new.

"So much of our precious human energy is used to build places that either destroy nature or depress the soul. But we are inspired by beauty. We can use art and architecture to ennoble and enhance life."

Through the practice of rituals, ancient and contemporary, we can also experience an expansion of our souls and a connection with something greater than ourselves, Steinberg believes. She has reclaimed much of her religious heritage through study and ritual.

One such ritual involves a small spice box with cloves that her grandmother brought from Russia. "As my grandmother aged, the smell of the cloves became fainter. After she died, I added fresh cloves to the box and now use it in the ceremony it was intended for, *Havdalah*. *Havdalah*, which is Hebrew for 'separation,' is the ceremony that separates the Sabbath and holidays from the rest of the week. Spices in a spice box, a braided candle, wine, songs and blessings are integral to the ceremony."

But before such rituals and ceremonies can stir us spiritually, Steinberg believes that we need to recognize that the irrational can make sense and that time is extremely fluid.

If you can give up the sense that life is a linear journey and see there is another dimension to life where time is not linear but eternal, then you can begin to put the spiritual component back into your life. This is theoretically what we do when we do rituals over and over again. We have life cycle rituals with living

and dying and with children coming of age, but our regular rituals of meditating, praying and lighting candles for the Sabbath are also meant to help us feel connected to eternal time. With these rituals, you can see your family not only at this particular point in time, but connected to all of history and to all families that have ever done this. You see yourselves as part of this eternal continuum that doesn't have a sense of the linear.

It's kind of an "ah-ha" experience. We often do our rituals in anticipation of the "ah-ha" experience. And I had it once. Before you get married in Jewish tradition, you go to a mikveh, the ritual bath. One of my classmates was a regular user of the mikveh, and I went with her to one in Manhattan.

I remember thinking, "Why am I doing this? I take a shower every day. What is the difference?" But in the middle of the experience, I had this flash: "This is what Jewish women have been doing for thousands of years." And suddenly it wasn't just me in the spring of 1976, but I had this really intuitive sense that this was one experience of all Jewish women. At that moment I experienced the power of that ritual. It confirmed my beliefs. And in this world, it's very hard to get that kind of confirmation. Instead we get material confirmations about buying a car, sending our child to summer camp, doing a good job or having a good idea.

Now I hope the rituals and interpretations I do will enable someone to have a good Jewish experience. I hope they have power and can give someone's life more meaning. For me, my experience was a moment of tremendous connecting up to that power. And then it went away. But like a dream, I still carry the memory of it.

"I like the Jewish tradition of Tikkun olam, which means fixing the universe or world. It is a huge subject within Judaism. One engages in acts of Tikkun olam whether or not one is internally motivated or spiritually moved. We hope if you do enough acts of Tikkun olam in the world you will get internal, spiritual motivation. It is a classic Jewish concept that through these acts, you hear the voice of wisdom or of God."

MARY JACKSTEIT
and
ADRIENNE KAUFMANN

Codirectors of The Common Ground
Network for Life and Choice

"Building common ground gives a sense of hope. You are offering an image of what is possible that starts to push against the pictures of relentless warfare. That will play out in ways you can't ever foresee."
—Mary Jacksteit

"As people get ready to leave for the day, we have them generate a word picture of how the day was for them. One person who really stands out in my mind is a woman who said, 'When I thought of coming today, I pictured it like a wall of oozy, gooey, yucky slime, and I thought I would be asked to put my hand through that wall. And when I did, I found a hand on the other side, reaching out to me.'"
—Adrienne Kaufmann

Albert Einstein once said that you can't solve a problem on the same level at which it originated. His sense of transcending conflict to seek solutions is evident in the work of The Common Ground Network for Life and Choice. Based in Washington, D.C., and gaining grassroots momentum from St. Louis to Cleveland to Pensacola, Common Ground allows those caught up in one of the most divisive issues of our times—abortion—to meet and talk with one another in a nonhostile way. In doing so, Common Ground helps communities begin to heal the hatred, bitterness and judgment typically clinging to this controversy.

"When two people publicly known as enemies give each other a hug as they leave a day of dialogue, or share addresses and telephone numbers with enthusiasm, that is a transformative experience. The whole image of yeast comes to mind. When enough people have had an alternative experience, it can have a transforming effect on our society," says Adrienne Kaufmann, Common Ground codirector.

Kaufmann, a Benedictine sister, and Mary Jacksteit, a lawyer, are a job-sharing team at the head of Common Ground. To ease the gulf between pro-life and pro-choice factions, they provide workshops, conferences, manuals and guidance aimed at helping typically opposing forces discover areas of common concern.

Working within a framework of ground rules, Common Ground participants explore the stereotypes, perceptions and misperceptions about one another. They share personal experiences and beliefs. They also learn new tools for relating, such as active listening or connective thinking, says Jacksteit. "We listen to the other person for that bit of wisdom or truth, for that something with which we can resonate or that we want to remember. This form of listening differs from listening for what you can rebut or disprove. People often comment about how this kind of experience is empowering. They say, 'If I can learn how to listen to people who seem so different from myself and appreciate them as human beings, I can do anything.'"

Remarkable alliances have been formed by former adversaries. In the St. Louis Common Ground effort, pro-choice and pro-life representatives lobbied together before the Missouri Legislature for support for disadvantaged and drug-addicted women and their children and for single-parent households.

Both Jacksteit and Kaufmann feel their work is part of their personal spirituality. As a Benedictine sister, Kaufmann feels acutely the call to help build a sense of community. "That is the Benedictines' primary reason for being. As I look around, I see that the spirit of community doesn't exist between pro-choice and pro-life people."

When she was a politically active college student, Jacksteit knew she wanted to do "what was right" in her life and career. "That sense of doing right has changed over time and taken on a more spiritual sense than when I was younger. I can't do the extracurricular spiritual life, squeezing in a little bit of spirituality at 10:15 at night. I have chosen to understand my work as a spiritual vocation. I ask, 'God, what is it I should be doing in the world?' and choose my work with that in mind."

MARY JACKSTEIT: *There is a lot of hopelessness and resignation and a sense of despair today about the ability of not only our country, but of human beings in general to cope with deep differences. I see our work as trying to create hope. We don't have to feel this way. We don't have to be resigned forever to having enemies and being at war. We can have hope if we choose to. We can look at one another in a different way and things can happen beyond what we ever imagined. Love is powerful if we choose to operate in that context.*

There is good in the world and there is evil. You are either making the world more loving or less loving. I am a Christian, and people often say Christianity is unworldly and impractical. But I find, as I get older, that it is absolutely so verified by experience. If what you do is life-destroying or community-destroying or denies the humanity of another person, those actions are not like a vapor that disappears and has no consequences. In your life, in the history of humankind, those actions do have consequences. People often do terrible things in the name of justice or because they feel they are right. But it is not adequate to say, "Well, I can do anything, because I am doing right, so it doesn't matter how I treat other people."

Recently, when I looked at a passage of Scripture, 1 Corinthians, chapter 13—which talks about love—it really struck me because it goes through a whole laundry list. It says you can give to the poor, you can speak like an angel, you can burn your body as a sacrifice—you can do all these wonderful things—but if you do them without love, they're nothing. For me that is such a profound truth. It matters so deeply how we live our lives and what we do in terms of relating to others. That is one of the powerful truths that underlies our work. To me, living a spiritual life is taking full responsibility for living the spiritual truths you know, and integrating the spiritual and the secular.

You can feel the absence of spirituality in a community when people feel their relationships or their sense of connection with one another is broken. Our efforts will be successful if we can help relationships form between people that would otherwise not exist. If people can feel connected, hug, exchange phone numbers or simply say, "I can't quite look at the situation as I did before," our efforts will have fruit.

Our society can and needs to go forward with a sense that we can live peacefully, justly and respectfully with our conflicts, viewing them as creative opportunities and not destructive forces driving us apart. If we can share some wisdom about that, based on our experiences, and offer that wisdom as a set of tools or a vision of hope, that is my ultimate goal.

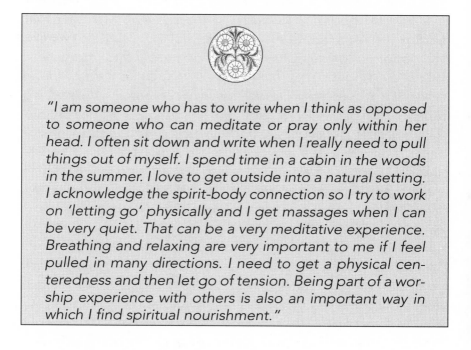

"I am someone who has to write when I think as opposed to someone who can meditate or pray only within her head. I often sit down and write when I really need to pull things out of myself. I spend time in a cabin in the woods in the summer. I love to get outside into a natural setting. I acknowledge the spirit-body connection so I try to work on 'letting go' physically and I get massages when I can be very quiet. That can be a very meditative experience. Breathing and relaxing are very important to me if I feel pulled in many directions. I need to get a physical centeredness and then let go of tension. Being part of a worship experience with others is also an important way in which I find spiritual nourishment."

ADRIENNE KAUFMANN: *I can define spirituality by its absence more than its presence. When I am on college campuses, there are a certain number of students who don't sense a connection with one another. They are wandering, and "Me, myself and I" is all they have. I find myself saying, "They are longing for spirituality," which for me is a sense of a real and vital connection to that which is bigger than myself. It is a sense of how each of us is related to a whole, and I name that whole God.*

I like to think of God as so big, so vast, so wonderful that no human person, not even all of creation, can capture God. But each of us is created in God's image in some way. Each of us reflects some piece of the total image of God. So when we want to experience our spiritual connections, we can remember that and try to discover the image of God in those with whom we live and work.

To me, spirituality is directly connected to the sense of brokenness in the bonds of our communities. What I experience with pro-choice and pro-life people is that they have cut themselves off from one another. In many cases, they have demonized and dehumanized and been so rude to one another that the bonds of community between them have been broken. Part of our work is to rebuild a space where pro-life and pro-choice people can share community and recognize they are each part of a larger whole. My ultimate dream would be to change the face of this conflict so the divisions are played out differently. This could make some contribution to overall society, changing the way public-policy decisions are developed: through dialogue rather than debate.

"I have a tape I made, a recording of my own voice, that centers me and reminds me of important things I want to remember. When I am in my car, on the Metro, going to bed or sometimes walking down the sidewalk, I play the tape. I need that external stimulus because I have a very flighty mind. One of the things I do on that tape is pull myself back to a memory of a time when I had a powerful experience of God's presence on the beach in Pensacola. I say, 'Go back there and remember God's saving, healing, ever-present love for you.' I go back and hear the seagulls and see the dawn spreading different colors in the sky, see the deep blue water contrasted with the sand, and I remember how I felt that particular day. It's very useful for me to remember God as ever-present in my life."

LINDA CALDWELL FULLER

Cofounder of Habitat for Humanity
and author

*"I have felt at times a Divine presence guiding me.
Sometimes when we have a problem, all of a sudden
the answer will just come, and it can't be only from me.
I think a lot of my thoughts are God-inspired."*

Thirty years ago, Linda Caldwell Fuller and her husband, Millard, were finalizing the blueprints for their dream house—a mansion on 20 acres, graced by swimming pool and horse stables. Today, the only blueprints the Fullers are concerned about are for the thousands of Habitat for Humanity homes built around the world each year.

The Fullers are one of the finest examples of the immense power of grassroots compassion. Since they cofounded Habitat for Humanity, the organization has expanded into more than 1,000 cities and thousands of homes. She couldn't have done her "soul work" these past decades without the organization's work, Fuller says.

"Spirituality really is so much more than loving yourself. It is more blessed to give than to receive. We get so much more back and experience such deep joy if we share with others outside of ourselves and our immediate family. That's my whole philosophy right there."

For her humanitarian efforts, Fuller has received the 1994 Harry S Truman Public Service Award, the "Gracious Ladies of Georgia" Award in 1993, the 1990 Temple Award for Creative Altruism from the Institute of Noetic Sciences, and the Berea College Service award. In 1990, she and her husband co-authored *The Excitement Is Building*, a book about Habitat for

Humanity's growth. She is also the editor of Habitat's first cookbook, *Partners in the Kitchen: From Our House to Yours.*

The mother of four children, Fuller freely shares her personal—and often painful—story of how one couple went from embracing the quintessential American dream to helping others realize their dream for a "simple, decent place to live." In 1965, Fuller and her husband were caught up in a consumption-in-overdrive lifestyle. A successful lawyer and entrepreneur, Millard seemed to make money almost effortlessly. Already millionaires, the Fullers owned shares in different business concerns, a 13-room house, a vacation retreat, two speedboats and a luxury car. But, only in her early 20s, Fuller painfully realized that her lavish, artificially constructed world was extinguishing her soul. She came to see that spiritual and psychological security aren't found in material comforts.

Millard came out of a lower middle-class family and decided at an early age that he wanted to be a millionaire. I came out of a middle-class family and had all I needed materially. But my mother made my clothes and we were very frugal. So I always wanted store-bought dresses. I never seemed to have enough shoes. My friends had much nicer things, so I always wanted more. And I wanted a big house.

When I met Millard I saw he had a real talent to make money. Together we went on this road of acquiring material possessions, and we did it very rapidly. After Millard graduated, he and a partner continued working day and night to build a company and within five years, they were both millionaires. That's when our marriage was really falling apart.

We had two children at the time, and he was not spending much time with them. But I had all the clothes I wanted. In fact, I had so many clothes, I had to move Millard's clothes out of the closet. We were driving a Lincoln Continental and were getting ready to build a mansion.

Then all of a sudden it dawned on me that nothing was really satisfying. I would buy a dress and it would please me for about three days. When I realized that we were about to lose our marriage, I wondered if we were on the right road. How could we get off this treadmill? That's when the big crisis came into our marriage. I was 24 and Millard was 30. I left him to take care of the children while I got counseling from a pastor in New York City for two weeks.

I didn't think that Millard would want to give up the business, but he came and said, "My family is more important. Let's just sell everything to my partner and start over." So we did. We also gave all of the money away. We didn't know what in the world we were going to do, but God led us to a Christian community in southwest Georgia, and that's where the idea of Habitat for Humanity started.

It was the best thing we could have done. If we had continued the way we were, we would have been either totally miserable or we would have divorced. Millard was physically ill and was even having a hard time breathing. Sores broke out on his ankles from stress. I guess a lot of people can be happy and rich at the same time. It just didn't work for us! We have lots of wealthy supporters of Habitat for Humanity, but they have balance in their lives. They know how to share what they have.

In 1995, we are finishing an average of 30 houses a day in 44 countries, which is about 10,000 houses a year. So the bottom line is homeowners get empowered and know they can do something about their situation. The people involved in Habitat for Humanity find they can express love by helping others find a decent place to live. It's very fulfilling and exciting work. We are always eager to get to the office. When we go to a house dedication, especially on a house we've helped to build, that just gives us the most wonderful feeling.

By being in contact with all the incredible numbers of volunteers and staff people, I have grown tremendously. They have provided a real source of inspiration to me. And working with President and Mrs. Carter has been absolutely amazing, very inspiring to me. Sometimes I just have to pinch myself when I *see how God has put my faith into action in such intangible and tangible ways.*

Unfortunately, apathy is a very paralyzing attitude in our society. It's an excuse to do nothing. What people don't realize is that if they don't remain paralyzed, and instead get out and help someone, they will feel great joy. Many people who have helped with Habitat for Humanity are discovering this deep-down joy.

In recent years, I have also discovered the joy in taking charge of things. I enjoy the freedom in planning how I want to spend my remaining years: helping others, dedicating a home, having my ideas and suggestions—or maybe I should say God's ideas and suggestions—accepted. I look forward to new hopes and challenges, to providing more environmentally sound and safe homes, to developing close friendships with people who are similar as well as different, to playing and smiling more and giving back at least a portion of what I've been given.

"Millard and I get out our calendar and mark out big blocks of time for us to get away. When we can get away to the beach or the mountains, relax, read and spend more time in prayer, that rejuvenates us. I think it is healthy to plan 'down time' when no activity is required. Or you can dust or do some menial tasks or play a game. I have a tendency to work too much. When I make time to relax, my work and life go better."

DAWN ENGLISH

Seattle foster mom
to more than 3,000 children

"If going to heaven requires a belief in a certain religion, I won't make it because I believe heaven is on earth. I believe what we do on earth the world mirrors back to us."

For some people, like Dawn English, living a spiritual life isn't about rigorous study or daily contemplation—it's about getting your hands dirty doing the work needed in the world. English has always felt that the most important thing in life is that we take better care of one another. And for English, a Seattle nurse, this philosophy isn't just rhetoric. In the past 28 years, she has taken care of more than 3,000 foster children, including three children with the AIDS virus. "We are responsible for our fellow man. We should be judged by how we treat other people. We're not worth anything if we haven't helped other people."

English says she entered into foster care for all the wrong reasons. "I was newly separated from my now ex-husband, and my own children were less than a year and five years old. They went to bed early, so I had a lot of time to sit around and feel sorry for myself. My sister went to a meeting where they talked about needing foster parents for teens, so I thought, 'I'll go into foster care and I won't have so much time to feel sorry for myself.' So I have to say my decision was really more to meet my needs than the children's."

Once English entered into foster care, she found she always had a full home. Literally, on some days, as one child left another would come through the door. She gradually created what she considers a family model, providing care for foster children of all ages. "That way I can take care of and hold a baby, for example, while I am talking to a teenager. So everyone's needs are met."

Included in English's family have been two infants and a teenager infected with HIV, the virus that causes AIDS. A *Time* magazine article on border babies whose mothers couldn't care for them because they were dying from AIDS spurred English to act. "I read this article and said, 'This is what I want to do.' In 1986, I contacted Social Services and asked them to let me care for any HIV babies."

While she waited for Social Services to call, English educated other foster parents and Red Cross and other volunteers about caring for HIV infants. Then one Friday evening in 1988, she got the call. "They said they had a nine-month-old with AIDS and her two-year-old sister. I already had a 'crack' baby, so I told them to call me back if they couldn't find a home. And they called back at midnight."

The two-year-old's mother chose to take her home, but English became the foster mother for the baby, Antonia. "She was only 10 pounds and could barely hold her head up. She could smile just a little bit. When I took her into our clinic, they thought she would die before she was a year old. "

Antonia is now six and, until this year when she became ill, has been a happy, strong child. English already knows the pain of losing one child to AIDS, a blue-eyed angel called Kayla.

When I first walked into Kayla's hospital room, she was all by herself, just this little girl with beautiful blond hair and big brown eyes holding onto her bottle. When I walked toward her crib, she threw the bottle away, tightened up her body, locked up her elbows and rigidly held herself away from me. And I thought, "Poor baby." So I took her home with me. I thought I would just give her a lot of love and care, and she would be just like Antonia. She would be fine.

What was most noticeable about Kayla was the emotional stuff. She had really never felt loved. Her mother didn't even know she herself was infected until she gave birth to this baby, who was infected, too. So Kayla had spent most of her life propped up in bed with a bottle as her mother got sicker. Her father passed her on from relative to relative and friend to friend. The only time anyone had even held her much was to hold her down to start an IV or give her some nasty medicine.

So the only control she had in her life was her bottle. She wouldn't eat. I think she thought, "If you are going to touch me, I will throw my bottle." It was such a challenge to let her know being loved was okay and contact was something we all needed.

I got her some stuffed animals and the softest blanket I could find. Being around the other kids I cared for was also good for her because she could see the other babies enjoyed being held. If I danced with one of them, Kayla would want to dance with me, too. It got to the point where she liked to sit in a walker at my knees and play with these little heart-shaped bracelets I had. She would take them off and put them on my fingers. And take them off and put them on. For hours. She didn't want to be held, but she wanted to be near me.

Finally, she would let me hold her with her bottle. She wouldn't drink from the bottle, but she would let me hold her with it. Then she got sick and had to be hospitalized. And instead of holding her stuffed animals or her blanket, which is what you'd expect kids to do when they are sick, she'd take this ring of keys and hold it for comfort. The hospital called me in the middle of the night and said they didn't think she was going to make it. I woke one of the kids and said, "I have to go to the hospital. Kayla is dying." And that was the first time I'd actually said the words. It was like a slap. I still thought she would be just like Antonia. Saying the words out loud was just such a shock.

But Kayla pulled through that time. And I stayed up all night talking to her doctor, who was just wonderful, about life and death and everything. I said, "She just needs more time. She needs more time, even another month. Then she would know I love her." And actually, we got another six weeks.

She got to the point where she would lay her head down on my shoulder and let me hold and rock her. Then she got sick again and went downhill fairly rapidly. So we admitted her to the hospital again. I took her blankets, stuffed animals and the "Nutcracker" music we used to dance to so she would have something from home.

At one point during the day, the doctor and nurses asked me to leave the room. I was in the waiting room with a volunteer from Shanti, a local agency that provides one-on-one emotional support to people affected by AIDS. Then I heard them call, "Cardiac arrest." And I just knew.

I went in, and they turned her ventilator off. I wrapped her in her blanket and held her on my lap, and she died in my arms. And that's what I wanted. If I could have had anything besides having her live longer, it was to have her die knowing we loved her.

"I do a lot. I know I do a lot. But I don't think I do enough. I feel bad sometimes because there is so much more I could do."

Contributors

SUSAN FORD BALES, Betty Ford Center board member and spokesperson for Breast Cancer Awareness Month.

JOAN BORYSENKO, mind-body scientist, psychologist, teacher and bestselling author of *Fire in the Soul: A New Psychology of Spiritual Optimism*, *Minding the Body, Mending the Mind* and many other books.

SOPHY BURNHAM, journalist, playwright and author of *A Book of Angels, Angel Letters* and other bestselling works. Executive Director of the Fund for New American Plays.

JOAN B. CAMPBELL, General Secretary, National Council of the Churches of Christ.

ADA DEER, senior-level policymaker, Washington, D.C., and a member of Wisconsin's Menominee Tribe.

BETTY EADIE, expert on near-death experiences and author of the bestselling *Embraced by the Light*.

MARIAN WRIGHT EDELMAN, founder and president, Children's Defense Fund, and author of *Measure of Our Success: A Legacy to My Children and Yours, Families in Peril: An Agenda for Social Change* and *Guide My Feet*.

DAWN ENGLISH, Seattle foster mom to more than 3,000 children.

MARILYN FERGUSON, human potential consultant, editor of the *Brain/Mind Bulletin* and author of *The Aquarian Conspiracy*.

BETTY FORD, former First Lady of the United States. Cofounder of the Betty Ford Center and author of *Betty: A Glad Awakening*.

LINDA CALDWELL FULLER, cofounder of Habitat for Humanity and coauthor of *The Excitement Is Building*.

NIKKI GIOVANNI, poet, English professor, and author of *Racism 101* and other books.

JANE GOODALL, scientist, humanitarian, author and founder of the Jane Goodall Institute.

JOAN HALIFAX, medical anthropologist, cultural ecologist, Buddhist teacher, author of *The Fruitful Darkness: Reconnecting with the Body of the Earth* and founder of Upaya, a Buddhist center in New Mexico.

NAOMI JUDD, entertainer, author of *Love Can Build a Bridge*, television producer and mind-body lecturer.

ADRIENNE KAUFMANN and MARY JACKSTEIT, codirectors of The Common Ground Network for Life and Choice, a national movement to widen understanding and tolerance between the pro-life and pro-choice movements.

ELISABETH KUBLER-ROSS, M.D., renowned expert on death and dying, and author of *On Death and Dying* and other works.

MADELEINE L'ENGLE, poet and author of 30 books, including *A Wrinkle in Time*.

CORINNE McLAUGHLIN, coauthor of *Spiritual Politics* and cofounder of Sirius, a spiritual community and ecological village in Massachusetts.

NELL NEWMAN, head of Newman's Own Organics.

CHRISTIANE NORTHRUP, M.D., holistic gynecologist, founder of Women to Women and author of *Women's Bodies, Women's Wisdom*.

RACHEL NAOMI REMEN, M.D., founder and director, Institute for the Study of Health and Illness. Medical director and cofounder of the Commonweal Cancer Help Program in California. Author of *Wounded Healers*. Assistant clinical professor of Family and Community Medicine, University of California, San Francisco, School of Medicine.

ELIZABETH ROBERTS, ecological teacher, consultant, and author of *Earth Prayers* and other books.

ARDATH RODALE, chairman and chief executive officer of Rodale Press. Author of *Climbing Toward the Light: A Journey of Growth, Understanding and Love*.

BONNIE STEINBERG, spiritual leader, Temple Isaiah of Great Neck, Long Island, New York.

ALEXANDRA STODDARD, interior designer and bestselling author of *Making Choices: The Joy of a Courageous Life, Living Beautifully Together* and other works.

FRANCES VAUGHAN, transpersonal psychologist, dream analyst, and author of *Inner Arc* and other works.

TERRY TEMPEST WILLIAMS, naturalist, writer, environmental activist, and author of *Refuge: An Unspoken Hunger* and other books.

Bibliography

These books have been valuable during my spiritual growth. Many were written by the women featured in this book.

Anderson, Sherry Ruth and Patricia Hopkins. *The Feminine Face of God: The Unfolding of the Sacred in Women.* New York: Bantam Books, 1991.

Berends, Polly Berrien. *Coming to Life: Traveling the Spiritual Path in Everyday Life.* San Francisco: HarperSanFrancisco, 1990.

Borysenko, Joan. *Fire in the Soul: A New Psychology of Spiritual Optimism.* New York: Warner Books, 1993.

————. *Guilt Is the Teacher, Love Is the Lesson.* New York: Warner Books, 1990.

————. *Minding the Body, Mending the Mind.* New York: Bantam Books, 1988.

Burnham, Sophy. *A Book of Angels.* New York: Ballantine Books, 1990.

Bynner, Witter, trans. *The Way of Life According to Lao Tzu.* New York: Capricorn Books, 1944.

Daniel, Alma, Timothy Wyllie, and Andrew Ramer. *Ask Your Angels.* New York: Ballantine Books, 1992.

Eadie, Betty. *Embraced by the Light.* Placerville, California: Gold Leaf Press, 1992.

Easwaran, Eknath. *Formulas for Transformation.* Petaluma, California: Nilgiri Press, 1977.

Edelman, Marian Wright. *The Measure of Our Success.* Boston: Beacon Press, 1992.

Foster, Richard J. *Freedom of Simplicity.* San Francisco: HarperSanFrancisco, 1981.

Gordon, Anne. *A Book of Saints: True Stories of How They Touch Our Lives.* New York: Bantam Books, 1994.

Guiley, Rosemary Ellen. *The Miracle of Prayer.* New York: Pocket Books, 1995.

Huffington, Arianna. *The Fourth Instinct: The Call of the Soul.* New York: Simon & Schuster, 1994.

Kwok, Man-Ho, Martin Palmer, and Jay Ramsay. *The Illustrated Tao Te Ching.* New York: Barnes & Noble, Inc., 1994.

Lindbergh, Anne Morrow. *Gift from the Sea.* New York: Vintage Books, 1955.

MacLaine, Shirley. *Going Within: A Guide for Inner Transformation.* New York: Bantam Books, 1989.

McClure, Vimala. *The Ethics of Love: Using Yoga's Timeless Wisdom to Heal Yourself, Others and the Earth.* Willow Springs, Missouri: Nucleus Publications, 1992.

McLaughlin, Corinne and Gordon Davidson. *Spiritual Politics.* New York: Ballantine Books, 1994.

Moore, Thomas. *Care of the Soul.* New York: HarperCollins, 1992.

————. *Meditations on the Monk Who Dwells in Daily Life.* New York: HarperCollins, 1994.

Morse, Melvin, with Paul Perry. *Closer to the Light: Learning from the Near-Death Experiences of Children.* New York: Ivy Books, 1990.

Occhiogrosso, Peter. *Through the Labyrinth: Stories of the Search for Spiritual Transformation in Everyday Life.* New York: Penguin, 1991.

Peck, M. Scott. *Further Along the Road Less Traveled: The Unending Journey Toward Spiritual Growth.* New York: Simon & Schuster, 1993.

Rilke, Rainer Maria. *Letters to a Young Poet.* Translated by Joan M. Burnham. San Rafael, California: New World Library, 1992.

Siegel, Bernie S. *Peace, Love and Healing.* New York: HarperCollins, 1989.

Smith, Huston. *The Illustrated World's Religions: A Guide to Our Wisdom Traditions.* San Francisco: HarperSanFrancisco, 1994.

Stoddard, Alexandra. *Daring to Be Yourself.* New York: Avon Books, 1992.

————. *Grace Notes.* New York: Avon Books, 1993.

————. *Living Beautifully Together.* New York: Avon Books, 1989.

————. *Making Choices: The Joy of a Courageous Life.* New York: William Morrow & Co., 1995.

Welwood, John, ed. *Ordinary Magic: Everyday Life as Spiritual Path.* Boston and London: Shambhala Books, 1992.

White Eagle. *The Quiet Mind.* Great Britain: The White Eagle Publishing Trust, 1972.

Williams, Terry Tempest. *Refuge: An Unnatural History of Family and Place.* New York: Vintage Books, 1991.

Williamson, Marianne. *Illuminata.* New York: Random House, 1994.

————. *A Return to Love: Reflections on the Principles of a Course in Miracles.* New York: HarperCollins, 1992.

————. *A Woman's Worth.* New York: Random House, 1993.